Nabanna

Bijon Bhattacharya (1915–1978) was born in Faridpur, in what is now Bangladesh and he moved to Calcutta in 1930. He became one of the founding members of the Indian People's Theatre Association (IPTA) in 1943. His most famous play that was performed by the IPTA was *Nabanna* (1944). After quitting the IPTA in 1948 he continued to write, direct and act in plays, write screenplays and act in films. Some of the more well-known plays by him include *Mara Chand* (*Dead Moon*, 1951) and *Debi Garjan* (*The Call of the Goddess*, 1966). He acted in films like *Meghe Dhaka Tara* (*Cloud-clapped Star*, 1960), *Subarnarekha* (*Golden Line*, 1962) and *Padatik* (*Foot Soldier*, 1973).

Arjun Ghosh is an Associate Professor at the Department of Humanities and Social Sciences, IIT Delhi, where he teaches courses on Indian and world theatre, performance theory and practice, authorship and copyright, and the future of writing. He was formerly Fellow at the Indian Institute of Advanced Study, Shimla. His previously published works include *A History of the Jana Natya Manch: Plays For the People* and *Freedom from Profit: Eschewing Copyright in Resistance Art*.

Nabanna

Of Famine and Resilience: *A Play*

Bijon Bhattacharya
Translated by ARJUN GHOSH

with essays by
Sova Sen, Tripti Mitra, Shombhu Mitra

RUPA

Published by
Rupa Publications India Pvt. Ltd 2018
7/16, Ansari Road, Daryaganj
New Delhi 110002

Sales centres:
Allahabad Bengaluru Chennai
Hyderabad Jaipur Kathmandu
Kolkata Mumbai

Nabanna and Production Note © Tathagata Bhattacharya 2018
Translation and introduction copyright © Arjun Ghosh 2018

Grateful acknowledgement is made to the following
for permission to translate copyright material:
Bishnupriya Dutt for '*Nabanna* and Me' by Sova Sen
Saoli Mitra for 'Memories' by Tripti Mitra
Saoli Mitra for the interview of Shombhu Mitra

Nabanna is a work of fiction. Names, characters, places and incidents are either the product of the author's imagination or are used fictitiously and any resemblance to any actual person, living or dead, events or locales is entirely coincidental.

All rights reserved.
No part of this publication may be reproduced, transmitted,
or stored in a retrieval system, in any form or by any means,
electronic, mechanical, photocopying, recording or otherwise,
without the prior permission of the publisher.

ISBN: 978-93-5304-028-4

Second impression 2019

10 9 8 7 6 5 4 3 2

Printed at Thomson Press India Ltd.

This book is sold subject to the condition that it shall not,
by way of trade or otherwise, be lent, resold, hired out, or otherwise
circulated, without the publisher's prior consent, in any form of
binding or cover other than that in which it is published.

Contents

Introduction	1
Characters	31
Act One	**33**
Scene One	33
Scene Two	41
Scene Three	48
Scene Four	56
Scene Five	61
Act Two	**72**
Scene One	72
Scene Two	83
Scene Three	91
Scene Four	97
Scene Five	103
Act Three	**115**
Scene One	115
Scene Two	119

Act Four | **128**
    Scene One | 128
    Scene Two | 143
    Scene Three | 149

Production Note for *Nabanna*, Bijon Bhattacharya | **158**
***Nabanna* and Me, Sova Sen** | **163**
Memories, Tripti Mitra | **170**
Interview, Shombhu Mitra | **177**
Cast | 187

Bibliography | 189
Endnotes | 193
Acknowledgements | 201

Introduction

In January 1944, in the midst of the Second World War, leading Indian industrialists met to draw up a set of proposals for the development of the Indian economy after Independence—the 'Bombay Plan'—to advocate an interventionist state in Independent India. Short of capital themselves, these industrialists wanted the central government to put in place basic industries and even signalled a willingness to accept a 'temporary eclipse' in 'freedom of enterprise' taking lessons from the 'Russian experiment'.[1] This plan was quite akin to the Nehruvian model of a planned economy which gave impetus to Indian industrial growth through state-led capital investment and tariff-based protections. The ideas that the elite used to govern India and manage the Indian economy maintained a remarkable continuity upto three decades after Independence. In fact, we can identify other instances where an idea, which took shape in the final years of colonial rule, continued in relevance after independence. The food crisis of the 1940s resulted in the institution of the practice of rationing of food. This was a dry run for the public distribution system in later decades. But if there was rationing to control distribution of food, an inefficient system run by an unresponsive government meant that there was also a violation of rationing provisions. This gave rise to hoarding and speculation in food items. The Bangla vocabulary saw the introduction of a new term—'kalobajari' or 'blackmarket'. The blackmarket and speculation in food items, unfortunately continues much beyond Independence, almost seventy years later. A similar continuity, though in a non-mechanized sector, was to be seen in the dominant ideas that governed the Indian theatre and much of India's cultural scape in the decades after Independence. The formation of the Indian People's Theatre Association (IPTA) in 1942 marked a series of experiments in the theatre and other performing arts that departed from the practices of the contemporary commercial stage. Set up with the motto of 'taking theatre to the people', the IPTA, along with other similar organizations, actively pursued an aesthetic goal of seeking a fresh idiom of conversing with an audience beyond the urban centres by working on traditional forms and adapting them for contemporary themes. Under the IPTA, theatre moved away from the control of the theatre managers and producers into a domain that empowered the artists— away from a star system towards a structure that emphasized collective functioning. While the broad emphasis on the group as the principal organizing structure still remains the mainstay in Indian theatre, the objectives as underlined by the IPTA in the 1940s held resonance over the sphere of Indian cultural creations even beyond the theatre for about three decades following Independence. Created in 1944, the production of *Nabanna* (The Harvest Festival) has been regarded by chroniclers of Indian theatre as a watershed play that encapsulated the IPTA experience.[2]

Calcutta in the 1940s

Nabanna sketches the predicament of peasants who faced the brunt of the famine that ravaged Bengal in 1943–44. Though the principal characters in the play are the peasants, the play itself was conceptualized and produced in Kolkata. As a refuge from the famine, hundreds of rural people walked to Kolkata to seek some form of sustenance. But Kolkata of the 1940s was a prime city of a colonial India—a space that was marked by the inequalities that colonial rule institutes and deepens through its structures of governance and control. *Nabanna* is simultaneously a chronicle of these injustices and an attempt to challenge them. In 1939, when the World War began, the Calcutta Improvement Trust was implementing large projects that undertook significant alteration of the cityscape. This included improvement of the aesthetic appeal by creating new parks, laying out pavements and street lamps and other street furniture. It also undertook a large project of demolitions to clear the way for what was to become the Central Avenue—an arterial road through the city. New apartment blocks were being created around the Central Avenue—an area which was rapidly occupied by the Marwari business families which chose to avoid the congestion around Burrabazar. The Marwari Association welcomed the clearing of slums in Burrabazar. The decongestion and beautification plans received support from the Bengal National Chamber of Commerce. Such plans were also welcomed by nationalist politicians like Bipin Chandra Pal who wanted the 'City Fathers' (i.e. the British administrators) to turn Calcutta into the 'City Beautiful'. However, there is no record of any response or opinion being sought from those that were most affected by the demolition works—the slum dwellers and the urban poor.[3]

War and Famine

This unequal relationship—between the British administration, the colonial elite and the poor—set up the terms of space in which was played out the most conspicuous effect the War had on Bengal—the famine. Unlike what is generally assumed, the War was not the determining cause of the famine. Indeed, it saw a high deployment of allied troops in the eastern front which was facing the threat of Japanese invasion.[4] So the war did increase the appetite for food supplies diverted towards the troops. The Japanese takeover stopped the import of rice from Burma. Further, in October 1942, a series of cyclones and floods in the Gangetic Bengal reduced the rice crop by about a third and caused large scale loss of human and animal lives, and destruction of rural housing.[5] However, Amartya Sen has indicated that Bengal did have near enough food supply as buffer to ride the storm.[6] Yet, it was the complete lack of humanitarian effort that lay behind the famine. In pursuit of a disastrous 'Denial Policy', the government ordered the burning of standing crops, seizure of excess foodgrains and destruction of boats in the delta. This was done to ensure that foodgrains did not fall in the hands of the enemy in the event of a Japanese invasion.[7] It was a scorched earth policy that robbed Bengal of its buffer foodgrain stock. Import from other regions in the subcontinent was diverted to the War.[8] The government refused to permit food imports into India by sea.[9] Yet, it is not that the government capitulated wholly in the face of the war. It displayed a great degree of resolve in ensuring adequate supply of food for Calcutta's 'priority classes' who were vital to the wartime production. It diverted food supplies to officials, privileged groups and organized industrial workers.

The Calcutta middle-class accessed from controlled price shops. During these times, Calcutta saw a new breed of food suppliers and speculators leading to hoarding of foodgrains.[10]

This diversion of food away from the hungry resulted in what has been called 'one of the more catastrophic, though least publicized, holocausts of the Second [World] War'.[11] The death toll in the famine outnumbered the Indian casualties in the War. While an estimated 30,000 Indian soldiers died in the War, the official figure for deaths doled out by the Famine Inquiry Commission was 'about 1.5 million'. Sen has demonstrated that this is a gross underestimate and the real figure is more than double that.[12] With all surplus rice cleared out, soon after the floods, the districts of South Bengal were left hungry and starving. The news of food stocks being available in Calcutta soon spread. Lakhs of rural destitutes trekked to the city and by July 1943 the streets were full.[13] The largest group—almost 41 per cent—of destitutes were those of agricultural labourers.[14] With controlled price shops unable to reign in skyrocketing prices of rice, most of the middle class budget was spent on food. The hungry and the starving, however, were left to procure food from the gruel kitchen.[15] But the supply did not meet the demand and the starving migrants first found themselves hunting for rice, then for just the starch from cooked rice—cries of 'phyan dao, phyan dao' rent the city lanes and bylanes. Even in the face of utter destitution, the migrants looked for rice and not cooked food as it was a denial of their human dignity to beg for cooked food—'we are farmers, not beggars'.[16] Even though they found shops well stocked with rice charging exhorbitant rates, there were no reports of arson. While there were reports of rice hoards—like the heaps of grain in the botanical garden covered with tarpaulin—the starving people dropped to death on the streets. Death was ubiquitous. As dead bodies piled up, the British administration promulgated the Bengal Destitute Persons (Repatriation and Relief) Ordinance in October 1943. Corpse disposal vans that were procured by the government to collect casualties from possible Japanese air raids were put into action. They picked up the sick, the starving and the 'living dead' at random and deposited them in repatriation camps outside Calcutta.[17]

Throughout, the colonial government existed in denial of the humanitarian crisis and the human-led causes of the catastrophe. *The Statesman* undertook a campaign to draw public attention to the crisis by publishing reports and photographs of the death that had hit the streets of Calcutta. But that was unable to move the British government. Then British Prime Minister Winston Churchill was quoted as saying, 'I hate Indians. They are a beastly people with a beastly religion.' The famine was their own fault, he declared at a war-cabinet meeting, for 'breeding like rabbits.'[18] It looked upon the crisis as a failure of public relations. They sought to contain the damage by imposing censorship on the press—English and Bangla.

Communists and the War

Nabanna addressed this apathy. However, for historical reasons, the play did not direct its ire towards the British government. Clearly, a stated indictment of the British government would have meant a very short life for the play—for as we shall find later in this essay, the script of the play did raise eyebrows at Lalbazar—the police headquarters of Calcutta. Beyond the censorship, the reason for *Nabanna* letting the colonial government off lightly lay in the political strategy of the Communist Party of India

(CPI). The War marked a new phase in the advancement of the Communist Party in India. Until the war, the Communist Party was forced to work underground or through the left-wing of the Congress party. The Nazi invasion of the Soviet Union in June 1941 and the fact that Britain was the only ally of a beleaguered Soviet Union, forced the CPI to rethink its opposition to what it termed till then, 'the imperialist war'. After months of deliberation, the CPI decided to call for support to what was now a 'people's war' against fascist aggression. The threat of a Japanese invasion of eastern India was real—the first Japanese bombs were dropped on Calcutta in December 1943.[19] The call of anti-fascism was part of an international coalition of artists and intellectuals who worked to deepen the resistance against fascist aggression of Hitler, Mussolini and Franco. In India, leaders like Jawaharlal Nehru tried hard to negotiate within the Congress for support towards the Allied war effort. Rabindranath Tagore sought for news from Russia even in his death bed in August 1941 for he believed that the Soviets alone would be able to halt the 'monsters'.[20] The CPI's support for the War effort in the face of the nationalist aggression in the form of the Quit India Movement prompted the lifting of the ban on the Party. This led to a situation where other than the communists, most leaders of other parties were behind bars.[21] The membership of the CPI rose drastically—4,000 in 1942; 15,000 in May 1943; 53,000 in mid-1946; and over 1 lakh by February 1948.[22] Such rise in strength, however, did not come easily for the CPI. It did have to contend with opposing the Quit India Movement at a time when there was an upsurge of anti-British sentiments. Also, much of the energy of the CPI in Bengal was expended in generating public opinion against the Japanese. This at a time when Subhas Chandra Bose had allied with the Japanese and led the Indian National Army (INA) in a bid to liberate India. Bose, who was a hero for many Bengalis, was termed a 'quisling' by the CPI.

Formation of the IPTA

It was the work put in by the cultural activists affiliated to the CPI that helped the communists overcome that political isolation. Following an international trend in the 1940s, a large number of artists, writers and intellectuals were attracted towards socialism. The Progressive Writers' Association (PWA), which had been formed in 1936, identified a triple threat—imminent fascist threat over India in the form of the advancing Japanese forces, the Macaulayan theories which denigrated Indian art and culture, and right-wing attempts to impose a reactionary definition of Indian culture.[23] The emphasis was on accentuating class struggle and using culture in widening socialism. In Bengal, Anti-Fascist Writers' and Artists' Association included, in its fold, workers from Calcutta tramways and jute mills. The move towards the performative arts was taken up by the students involved in the Youth Cultural Institute (YCI) formed in 1940. The YCI took to group singing. These organizations designated among their tasks the inculcation of progressive values among the people and actively prepared the people as recipients for their literature. It encouraged the opening of bookshops, small libraries, establishment of night schools and carrying out of literacy campaigns. As an association, the PWA also stood for the protection of the rights and interests of writers at the hands of exploitative printers and publishers.

The members of the YCI were influenced by socialist plays in English like Clifford Odet's *Waiting for Lefty* which was performed by the Institute at the conference of the Students' Federation in Patna in December 1941.[24] But neither were there socialist plays in Bangla nor did the contemporary stage offer any scope for staging such plays. That is when the members of the YCI started writing their own plays, first in English and then in Bangla.[25] The YCI's first play in Bangla was *Anjangarh* (1940).[26] In *Anjangarh* and *Kerani* (1940) the attempt was to practise collective playwriting—there would be no public disclosure of the playwright's identity.[27]

The increasing inclination towards the performing arts within the YCI and the Anti-Fascist Writers' and Artists' Association led to the formation of the IPTA on 25 May 1943 at the Bombay Marwari School in the side lights of the conference of the CPI.[28] There was a concerted effort from the CPI to create a platform of artists who could articulate the position of the communists before the people. The poet Subhas Mukhopadhyay explains that it was perhaps easier for the CPI to attract writers and artists to its affiliate organizations due to the general apathy among the Congress and other swadeshi organizations about the role of writers and artists in the sphere of politics.[29] It was during this recruitment drive that Shombhu Mitra and Bijon Bhattacharya involved themselves in the activities of the IPTA.[30] Some of the other artists who were involved in the IPTA at this time were Sova Sen, Tripti Mitra, Sajal Roychowdhury, Rabindra Majumdar, Anu Dasgupta and Kalyani Mukherjee. Shombhu Mitra noted that the IPTA did not have any restrictions on taking artists and enthusiasts in its fold on ideological grounds.[31] While some of them were attracted by the idea of escaping the restrictions of the commercial stage, others joined the IPTA enthused by its ideological inclinations. There were still others who were political activists who discovered their creative side while within the IPTA. This would often create a tug of war between two affiliate organizations. While the IPTA wanted Benoy Roy's songs in Bombay, the trade union wanted him to lead the jute workers' agitation in Calcutta. Benoy Roy did sing in Bombay.[32]

As mentioned earlier, this group of young artists was aware of contemporary trends in European drama, as well as reading writers like Lenin, Ralf Fox, Stephen Spender, Israel Epstein and Lu Shun.[33] However, the existing plays in Bangla neither spoke of the concerns of the poor and the oppressed nor did they reflect the ideological concerns that these artists shared. As an attempt to prepare new scripts, the CPI mouthpiece *Janajuddha* (People's War) announced a playwriting competition calling for anti-fascist plays. The competition was readvertised in *Arani* on 23 April 1943. The competition failed to generate a good response. So the writers of the IPTA decided to write their own plays—each of them were to write a short play which would then be read collectively. As part of this effort, Manoranjan Bhattacharya wrote *Homeopathy*, Benoy Ghosh wrote *Laboratory* and Bijon Bhattacharya wrote *Agoon* (Fire). In May 1943, *Agoon* and *Laboratory* were performed. *Agoon* was directed by Bijon Bhattacharya and *Laboratory*, by Shombhu Mitra.[34] The appreciation received by these two plays led Bijon Bhattacharya to write *Jabanbandi* (Testimony). *Jabanbandi* was performed along with *Homeopathy* a few months later. Produced at the peak of the famine and the occurrence of destitution in the streets of Calcutta, they were effective in increasing awareness about the factors behind the famine as well as generating contributions for relief. They would form part of a variety of items performed as part of a sequence at specific venues under the aegis of the Cultural Squad of the Bengal People's Relief Committee. Some of the other items that would be part of the sequence were the ballet theme 'Save Bengal' composed by Shanti Bardhan. It carried forward the experimental spirit of Uday Shankar's 'Rhythm of Life' and 'Labour and Machinery'.[35] The medley of songs—'Nabajibaner Gaan' (Songs for a New Age) by Jyotirindra Moitra put forward the interplay between various forces of formation, destruction, oppression and resistance.[36] Together with the songs of Benoy Roy they created a tradition of group music.[37] The various presentations reflected attempts at bold experimentation with forms to speak of an age which was riven with conflict, and political and social resistance. They also represented a consciousness among artists and writers who were stirred by the famine as well as the spirit of nationalism and anti-colonialism. Such consciousness stretched beyond the IPTA. In their art, Zainul Abedin, Somnath Hore and Chittaprasad recorded the human catastrophe behind the pervasive images of death and hunger. These images were carried in the Communist Party mouthpiece and helped generate an understanding of the magnitude of the famine at a time when the official narrative was one of denial.[38] The reactions to the famine are also captured in the fiction and poetry of the times. These lines by Premendra Mitra capture the poignancy and the loss of human dignity that the famine brought in:

> *Human-like, yet, not quite human,*
> *Cruel caricatures of humanity!*
> *Yet they move and speak,*
> *Like debris they pile up by the road,*
> *Sit, foraging food, on piles of garbage.*[39]

The discussions on experimentation on language and form began with *Agoon*.[40] The IPTA chose the realist mode to present and analyse the lived reality of the people and the issues faced by them. Language played a role in depicting realism. The attempt was to approximate the everyday language of the characters. *Agoon* experimented with an episodic plot. The episodic form suited the purpose of stringing together a series of situational actions as dramatized pamphlets. The scenes were held together around a single character and around the theme of famine and hunger. The anger and desperation of people from various strata of society were brought together in the queue before a Fair Price Shop. The experiment continued with *Jabanbandi* which presented a longer action in a single act. It was here that the story of a peasant family thrown to destitution by the famine and the social forces associated with it. They trek to Calcutta in search of food but the play ends with the death of the child of the family.[41] In performance, *Jabanbandi* marked a difference from contemporary stage traditions as no elaborate stage was used. Instead, there were a few pieces of furniture and symbolic properties. The performance received appreciation. The *Anandabazar Patrika* reviewed the performance of 3 January 1944 at the Star Theatre in Calcutta, 'Based on a set of issues…*Jabanbandi* was enjoyable. The costumes, the dialogue delivery and acting pleased the audience. To carry off a realistic depiction of peasant life on stage is not a small accomplishment.'[42] *Jabanbandi* created an acceptance of the depiction of the peasant on stage.[43]

At the time of the performance of *Jabanbandi*, there was a call for collecting money and material for famine relief.[44] Nemichand Jain translated *Jabanbandi* into Hindi. It was performed in Bombay by artists from Calcutta. The performance managed to raise about one lakh rupees.[45] The success of this effort caused the IPTA and the Communist Party to plan the development of a Central Squad of artists. At the same time the appreciation received by *Jabanbandi* caused the artists of the Bengal IPTA to take the next step on creating a full-length play around the theme of the famine. Shombhu Mitra was asked to join the Central Squad but he refused to do so as the creation of *Nabanna* was already in the offing.

Bengali Stage before *Nabanna*

In the early 1940s, religious and mythological plays dominated the Bengali stage. The theatre was highly individualistic and centred around stars.[46] Hitherto the tallest figures of the Bengali theatre—Ardhendu Sekhar Mustafi, Girish Ghosh, Shishir Bhaduri and others were principally interested in showcasing their own acting talent on the stage.[47] In fact, the story goes that once Shishir Bhaduri had boasted that if he recited the alphabet in the middle of the road, a crowd would gather to watch his performance.[48] And in the play the central character was almost always heroic, tall and handsome. Theatre owners would order playwrights to write according to their orders. It wasn't really a theatre for the ordinary people with ticket prices beyond their reach. The IPTA changed this order. It placed the common person at the centre of action. The principle of collective functioning meant that no one person would grab all the eyeballs. Sajal Roychowdhury tells us that actors in the IPTA were trained not to covet specific roles. The souvenir published on the occasion of the first performance of *Nabanna* spoke of a crisis in culture where the theatre houses were unable to meet the requirements of the audience and address the contradictions of contemporary society. The IPTA endeavoured to create theatre that would extend the boundaries of the theatre public both by enlarging its reach by taking its plays beyond the proscenium and also by extending the form and the idiom of its plays. The souvenir published on the occasion of the performance of *Tinti Natika* (Three Short Plays) in January 1944 criticized the view that those outside the learned society could not understand the theatre or did not want theatre. It announced that the IPTA's endeavour was to create plays that indicated social processes.[49] The IPTA in general and the production of *Nabanna* in particular, marked the transition from the dominance of the commercial theatre to the emergence of the theatre collective or Group Theatre.

The Creation of *Nabanna*

Born in Faridpur (now in Bangladesh), Bijon Bhattacharya's first experience with theatre was when he wrote a play for his fellow inmates at the hospital where he was undergoing treatment for tuberculosis. Later he wrote *Agoon* and *Jabanbandi*—each play an expansion of his skills. When the IPTA decided to create a full-length play based on the experience of *Jabanbandi*, Bijon Bhattacharya began a hunt for ideas. He was working as a journalist at the time. He recounted that he would walk back from work every evening and notice famine destitutes who lived on the streets on his way back. He would wonder if there was anything he could have done for them. One such evening, he followed the conversation of a couple who were not speaking of hunger or want, but of life back in their village, of the celebration of Nabanna (harvest festival) the previous year and the joys associated with it. As he passed that area again a few days later, he spotted a corpse—such corpses being usual on the streets of Calcutta in those months. He feared that the corpse might have belonged to the one whose story he had overheard the other evening. It was at this point that he decided on the theme for the new play—to let the characters tell their own story.[50] And he chose to let them tell that story in their own language.

In 1942–43, Bhattacharya had toured Khulna, Jessore and Basirhat and knew the language of the region well.[51] The action of *Nabanna* is set in Aminpur which is said to be in Medinipore. The language of the peasants in the play is a mix of the languages of Medinipore and Hooghly districts of Bengal. There is, however, no tradition of the celebration of Nabanna in Medinipore. Unlike *Jabanbandi* which ends in the death of Poran Mondol, in *Nabanna,* the festival indicates hope. During the writing of *Nabanna*, Bhattacharya's colleague Gangapada Basu returned from a visit to his village home. When Bhattacharya had asked him how the peasants were coping with the aftermath of the famine, Basu told him—though there was a lot of rice in the field, the peasants who were weak or depleted in numbers could not harvest the produce. So they had devised a method of harvesting each others' fields collectively.[52] This idea stuck by and Bhattacharya found the ending for his play—one that would allow the peasants to return to control of their lives, and find in solidarity a method of resistance to tyranny and hunger. The title of the play emphasizes this hope.

The Play

Nabanna begins with an action-filled scene referencing the Quit India Movement. Given that the CPI had opposed the Quit India Movement, the decision to begin the play with a reference to the movement tells us of the relative independence that the IPTA exercised in its work. In an interview to Samik Bandopadhyay, Bijon Bhattacharya claimed, 'We did not try to speak on behalf of the Party. We spoke on behalf of the people. Our job was to prepare the ground. Later the Party could sow the seeds.'[53] The Quit India Movement being a mass movement did galvanize the anti-colonial spirit of large sections of the people. By referencing the movement in the first scene, *Nabanna* chooses to develop a connect with the people. However, the treatment of the movement in *Nabanna* was not uncritical. Though not named, the figure of Judhisthir in the very first scene presents a leader of the movement. Judhisthir, not to be seen later in the play, comes across as a leader who is not involved in the action but provides directions. This scene was criticized to be anti-Congress.[54] A contrast to Judhisthir is the heroism of Panchanani who was one with the agitators. Her character was modelled on that of Matangini Hazra who heroically led a procession of volunteers to take over the Tamluk Police Station. When the police opened fire, she did not retreat and continued to implore the police not to fire on the crowd till she died of bullet wounds.

The second scene of the play introduces us to its principal characters—the villagers of Aminpur. Bijon Bhattacharya shows exceptional dramatic skill in wielding a new tradition on the Bengali stage—that of the collective hero. The scene shows the famine and hunger setting in and prepares the reader for the crisis brought about by the storm in the following scenes. While it is the villagers of Aminpur who gather in the final act to discover in collective harvesting an answer to the tyranny of the Haru Dutta-Kalidhan Dhara combine—the principal villains representing the conglomerate of the landowning classes, the moneylenders, the land grabbers, the traders and the hoarders—for the sake of continuity through the play, we follow the fortunes of the Samaddar family. Further, in order to maintain a link in the scenes featuring Haru Dutta and Kalidhan, Bhattacharya brings in Niranjan as a worker in Kalidhan's shop. Binodini narrates to Niranjan the events since he had left his village home—a link that allows Niranjan to connect with the predicament of his family. In the different scenes across Acts Two and Three, the play represents the various responses of the government and the middle-class of Calcutta to the influx of hungry, sick and dying people to the city. The presence and involvement of various members of the Samaddar family help the audience view the events and the victims of the famine with sympathy. At the charity clinic Pradhan's delirium is a sign of a deep insight. Here he carries on from the sarcastic humour when he allows himself to be photographed (II ii): 'Go sell pictures of this skeleton. Go! Go!' At the clinic when the doctor tells him that there is nothing wrong with him, he keeps repeating, 'There is no pain.' The city of Calcutta and its multifarious agencies are incapable of nursing Pradhan's pain—the pain of being reduced to a lesser than human creature. Denied food while trying to retrieve it from the bin, Kunja has to almost steal food from a dog (II iii). Even the dog bites back. It is Pradhan who converts his pain into wisdom and calls on the villagers to be prepared for the next storm and the next assault on their humanity in the final moments of the play.

On the one hand the play disbanded the claim of the British government who had tried to frame the invading Japanese as the only enemy responsible for the famine. It framed the administrators, the landlord class, the apathetic middle-class and the traders as class enemies of the peasantry. Playing before a Calcutta audience, it provided them with an alternative mode of responding to the incidence of death and dying all across the city. It is the character of the wedding guest—Nirmalbabu—who sounds a discord in the celebratory world of plenitude in which a large section of the middle-class existed: 'People who have money may hold such views! The trouble is that most people do not have that kind of money.' Nirmalbabu appeals to the sensitive Calcutta audience: 'Should we be silent in the face of injustice?' (II iii). Nirmalbabu is a guide to the Calcutta audience to articulate its response to the famine—to shake off apathy and adopt a critical view and participate in the relief effort.

On the other hand, the play restrained itself from a direct indictment of the British administration. The communists had only recently been allowed to function legally. There existed an environment of constant surveillance and censorship through provisions such as the Dramatic Performances Act 1876 which made the prior scrutiny of the script by the police mandatory for a permission to perform.[55] The predominant strategy of nationalist plays in the past was to take recourse to instances of bravery and martial prowess in mythology or in narratives celebrating vicarious exploits against real or imagined enemies. Even for the inclusion of the violence in the opening scene the playwright had some explaining to do. Bijon Bhattacharya had to justify the script to an Assistant Commissioner of Police at the headquarters of the Calcutta Police at Lalbazar.[56] Yet the script is only a part of the performance script. Much of the meaning generated in production exists between the performers and the spectators and can escape the scrutiny of the text. As Bijon Bhattacharya explained, in the first scene of the script, 'Instead of the sound of gunshots, we mentioned the clashing of bamboo sticks, the audience understood it, but the police could not.'[57] There is no direct implication of the British government for the famine and related instances of shortages and misgovernance. The doctor at the clinic only expresses his helpnessness at the lack of facilities and medicine but does not indicate who is responsible for this condition (III ii). For the sake of dramatic brevity, Haru Dutta and Kalidhan Dhara, the villains are also shown to be potential rapists and running an organized trafficking of young women. The arrest of the duo by the Inspector of Police could possibly have indicated an efficient and just administration. However, after the first performance, the leaders of the CPI among the audience suggested that it would be wrong and unrealistic to show the police to he honest and effective. Hence a change was made to the script where the arrested duo share knowing glances at each other which indicate that they can easily bribe the police and secure their release. In fact, this arrangement is pointed out earlier in the play when Kalidhan's collector tells the Bhadralok that the police cannot help in the procurement of rice as Kalidhan has 'purchased' many judges and magistrates (II i).

In Performance

Shombhu Mitra and Bijon Bhattacharya co-directed *Nabanna*. Shombhu Mitra was in charge of various aspects of production, while Bijon Bhattacharya was in charge of the action and training the actors in the language of the peasant characters.[58] Sudhi Pradhan and Chitto Banerjee assisted in various aspects of the production. There was a concerted effort to recruit women actors for the stage. Tripti Mitra who had already performed in *Jabanbandi* was Binodini; Sova Sen was Radhika. Bijon Bhattacharya made a special request to political activist Manikuntala Sen to perform as Panchanani. It was felt that it would take the experience of political activism to play the character on stage even though Sen did not have any previous experience of performing on stage.[59] The rehearsals were held at the IPTA office on Harrison Road in central Calcutta.

Veteran stage artist Manoranjan Bhattacharya suggested the use of jute cloth to create the principal stage design for the production. According to Shombhu Mitra, though some people thought of the use of jute as a 'proletarian touch', the actors themselves did not look upon it as a 'poor' material. They did like the colour and of course, it was cheap. The colour of jute had not been used on the Bengali stage and it marked a radical break from the tradition of detailed set designing. A lot of people were apprehensive of the use of the material.[60] Various symbols drawn on large sheets of paper were used on set to depict the particularities of a location—for instance, the picture of Ganesh indicated Kalidhan's shop; a piece of railing indicated the park.[61]

During the rehearsals there was deep anxiety and expectation among the actors and other members and supporters of the IPTA. Clearly, this was a play which continued on the path of experimentation that had been adopted by YCI and in the plays performed earlier by the IPTA. In fact, the atmosphere of apprehension was accentuated with a lukewarm response to the play on the day of the dress rehearsal.[62] The first performance of *Nabanna* was held at Srirangam theatre on 24 October 1944.[63]

Before the curtains went up Shombhu Mitra introduced the audience to the time of action of the first scene over a loud speaker from the backstage—'1942, 9th August.' When the curtains went up, the audience saw a reddened background with lit up torches and the sound of guns (created using clashing of bamboo sticks). The reddened background created silhouetted figures using mime action to depict the exciting events of the Quit India Movement.[64] Some critics felt that a play which begins with such a great degree of tension would be very difficult to sustain. However, *Nabanna* did not follow an Aristotelian structure. The four remaining scenes of the first act are set within the Samaddar household and have a modicum of continuity. But in the rest of the play, each scene plays out a different episode without a strong narrative continuity. The challenge before the production was to ensure a dramatic momentum through these episodes. It used the revolving stage of Srirangam to move swiftly from one scene to the other to ensure that the audience did not get emotionally involved in the action of any particular scene and their attitude remained one of critical view of the issues involved.[65] For the scenes which were set in Calcutta, cries of 'Phyan dao' from the backstage were inserted in the transition between scenes. These cries were still fresh in the minds of the Calcutta audience and helped in situating the action within their immediate experience.[66]

For the background score and sound effects a piano was used—played by Sujith Nath.[67] The use of light too left many traditionalists dumbfounded. The carbon arc was the only form of spotlight available. Back projection was used to create silhouetted images on the background screen. This was how the cattle racing was shown (IV iii). In the scene of the festival the women danced downstage with oil lamps balanced on their heads. There would be no light on them. Instead floodlights would be used from the wings onto the background screen creating a silhouette effect. The instructions surprised the light operator who exclaimed, 'What are you saying, shouldn't I put some spots on the actors?'[68] The light operator was picking up skills which would later be perfected by legendary light designer Tapas Sen—a technique where maximum drama could be created using minimal resources. Like the use of the revolving stage, the use of lights in *Nabanna* shows that the IPTA's use of technology may have been limited by resources but not by ideology or imagination.

Reactions and Legacy

The initial reactions to the production were mixed. Perhaps, the more effective immediate reactions were negative coming primarily from the theatre establishment. Stalwart of the Bengali stage Shisir Bhaduri felt, 'If the IPTA puts up these kinds of plays people will watch it for one or two days. But if we do it no one will come to watch. They will call it "beggars' theatre". Such theatre cannot survive without support from the government.'[69] Some of the reviews commented on the weakness of the script— of it being disjointed. The presence of women actors on stage along with 'half-naked' men also received negative opinion.[70] On the other hand, members of the cast have noted in their reminiscences that various members of the audience walked into the green room after the performance congratulating the artists. There were other reviews that were favourable and hailed the play for its innovations and the portrayal of peasant life on stage.[71] It would be wrong to claim that the remarkability of *Nabanna* was evident from the very first round of performances. The impact of the play was to be felt in the years and decades to come as the members of the production team moved forward to shape the Bengali theatre. On the occasion of the twenty-fifth anniversary of *Nabanna*, Nemai Ghosh claimed, 'For many of the stalwarts of the Bengali stage, the IPTA was a Theatre Institute and *Nabanna* was a major course.'[72] As mentioned earlier, the Bengali theatre practice of the next few decades would bear on it the mark made by the formative years of the IPTA—with its emphasis on collective performance through group theatre, the emphasis of a content that bore a critical relationship to society, and theatre that was non-commercial and drew on volunteer and amateur participation. Though the precursors to *Nabanna*, in the form of *Agoon, Laboratory* and *Jabanbandi* did prepare the ground for *Nabanna*, the fact that *Nabanna* was performed as a full-length play brought home the innovations and the break from tradition to the contemporary theatre establishment. Several commentators have remarked that it was perhaps this factor which caused the owners of commercial theatre to refuse to rent out their theatres to the IPTA thereafter. In doing so, they were not competing with the IPTA as the latter was a non-commercial entity. They were afraid of losing their business altogether due to a change in public taste.[73] However, the IPTA did perform *Nabanna* beyond the revolving stage of Srirangam.[74] Nemai Ghosh records a performance of the play before an audience of about five to six thousand at the Mohammed Ali Park in Calcutta.[75] The IPTA was invited to perform *Nabanna* at a Kisan Sabha Conference at Hatgobindopur. But a powerful storm meant the conditions were very difficult for performance on a makeshift stage. The actors decided not to perform. But the trade union leaders persuaded them to perform as about twenty-five thousand spectators had gathered for the show—'If you go away, the peasants would feel insulted that the urban actors went away while we waited for them in the rain.' The performance continued into the darkness using dock lights.[76] Sova Sen remembered another incident that occurred after one of the rural shows of *Nabanna*—'A small boy came to meet me in the makeup room. He had lost all his family in the famine. The [Communist] Party had rescued and rehabilitated him. He had saved some money in a box. He said he liked the previous day's performance a lot and that Radhika engaged in dehusking reminded him of his sister. He gave me all the money he had in the box. I have never received a greater prize in my entire life.'[77] Clearly *Nabanna* was not a play that appealed only to the middle-class audience of Calcutta. Unlike the contemporary Bengali theatre, *Nabanna* could appeal to a large section of audiences.

Realizing the potential for campaign and famine relief, the IPTA decided to adapt *Nabanna* into a full-length feature film in Hindi—*Dharti ke Laal* (1946). Directed by Khwaja Ahmed Abbas the cast of this film was drawn almost entirely from among the artists of the IPTA.[78]

Unfortunately, though the experience of performing *Nabanna* and other plays did leave a lasting legacy on the future of the Bengali theatre, the IPTA itself disintegrated soon after Independence. The overall confusion that Independence brought to the communist movement in India and the attitude of the CPI towards cultural organizations were in part responsible for the breakup. It responded by denigrating the achievement of political Independence and called for the heightening of the struggle for social and political emancipation. The CPI was banned soon after the Independence in 1948. The IPTA was forced to work underground. Samik Bandopadhyay retells a personal account of Karuna Bandopadhyay: 'There would be our men waiting at the mouth of the lane, ready to come rushing at the first signs of a police raid. We had to change the rehearsal site too, and it took people time to assemble at the site, for the location would be kept a secret till the last moment.'[79] One of the reasons that the IPTA managed to attract a wide spectrum of talent was the broadness in its attitude towards democratic and progressive values. However, as the political space for the CPI narrowed, it adopted a much narrower definition of political commitment. The cultural organizations began to be treated as rearguard of the Communist Party. The strongest indictment of the left-wing deviations of the Party in its running of the cultural front emerged in the form of a document titled 'On the Cultural Front' submitted to the CPI in 1954 by Ritwik Ghatak, then a member of the cultural front and the party, later a legendary film-maker: 'The Party generally sees the Cultural Front in two ways—one, as a "money-earning machine" (these are harsh words we know, but they just cannot be helped), and, two as a mobilizer in meetings and conferences to keep the crowd (and not masses) engaged with whatever the artistes can offer [...] It is very difficult to determine how much the Party cares for culture as the property of the people.'[80] Ritwik Ghatak was expelled from the Party in October 1955. Shombhu Mitra described an attitude of suspicion towards independent spirit of creativity: 'I had placed an opinion that we should have our own theatre and that it would help the movement. But that idea was criticized by some who said that this is what bourgeois artists do—they want their own set up.'[81] Given that many more opportunities opened up when the government of the independent nation set up cultural institutions, many artists no longer found the constricted space within the IPTA and allied organizations conducive.

After independence, *Nabanna* was performed several times by the Bohurupee theatre group in 1947–48 and in 1953. It was revived by Bohurupee in 1989 when the play was included as one of the classics of modern Indian theatre for the Nehru Natya Samaroh organized by the Sangeet Natak Akademi.

The IPTA initiated a lasting tradition of political theatre in India. It provided a platform which allowed artists the scope to train their creativity with a great degree of freedom, the only guiding light being the very basic humanist values. Of course, we cannot ignore the influence that the anti-colonial nationalism and the Soviet and Chinese revolutions had on the artists and activists in the 1940s. But ideology was not one that was handed down as a prescription by party apparatchiks. It was not as if the artists were sure of what they produced. The live link with trade unions and other mass organizations on the one hand and with the audience on the other hand, helped guide them through their experiments. They learnt through the experiences of various shorter plays under the YCI and then in *Agoon*, *Laboratory* and *Jabanbandi*. An atmosphere of shared creativity—very different from that of the commercial stage—allowed the artists to bring into the production their encounters with the world around them. We have already seen how Bijon Bhattacharya incorporated in *Nabanna* a conversation he picked up on the street. In an interview, Tripti Mitra recorded one of her lasting images of the famine:

> I used to reside in my uncle's house on Sadananda Road on the second floor… Probably we were not supposed to meet at the IPTA that evening. I noticed something from the window. There was a large house opposite ours with a portico. A lot of destitute people had taken shelter there. In those days in every kitchen the starch would be drained out after rice was cooked. The starch would flow out of the drainage pipe onto the footpath. The destitute…would place a pot at the drainage pipe to collect the starch and consume it. They collected starch from our house as well. We did not feel unusual about it. For it was happening all around. I saw someone came running towards our

house. I realized that our cook was draining the starch. After collecting the starch she—a girl—went back. It was not possible to guess her age. They were all just skeletal figures. But she did have three or four children. I saw the entire thing with my own eyes. I can't forget it even today. The moment she crossed back the children rushed towards her. But she chased them away, slapping some of them and started gobbling up the starch. I was shocked! I could not imagine such a thing. Then as she had consumed a fair bit, the children crying at a distance...she looked up. May be just a bit of starch remained. Three or four children. She started sobbing profusely. As if, why did I finish off the starch! I understood—there was so little starch that it was not enough for three or four children. I still remember that scene...[82]

Those among the middle-class who witnessed such sensitivity—those who did break free from the comfort of their 'priority class' convenience towards the life outside their windows—were driven by an urge to intervene. Some of them, like Tripti Mitra, took up a role in relief efforts. Others became activists. And some of them took to their creativity to give expression to the humanistic response to a human-created tragedy with a realization that acts of kindness were not enough. A systemic change was imperative.

Nabanna

Characters

Pradhan Samaddar	(Aged farmer of Aminpur)
Kunja Samaddar	(Pradhan's nephew)
Niranjan Samaddar	(Kunja's brother)
Makhan	(Kunja's son)
Panchanani	(Pradhan's wife)
Radhika	(Kunja's wife)
Binodini	(Niranjan's wife)
Dayal Mondol	(neighbour)
Haru Dutta	(local moneylender)
Kalidhan Dhara	(rice seller)
Rajib	(Kalidhan's collector)
Chander	(a farmer)
Judhisthir	(revolutionary)
Photographers	(newspaper representatives)
First bhadralok	(rice buyer)
Barakorta	(head householder)
Aged beggar	
Dom	
Inspector	
Doctor	

Digambar
Fakir
Khuki's mother
Beggar
Bengal Madonna

Bhadralok, Nirmal, Tout[83], Beggar, Haru Dutta's brother-in-law, Constable, Patient, Servant, Chander's daughter, Barkat, Farmer, starving people, crowds.

Act One

Scene One

As the day ends, the darkness of the night makes its slow descent upon this wretched village.[84] The stage is dark. The horizon in the background is tinged in red. In the dim light can be seen the silhouetted figures passing upon a plateaued mound. Enter two men. They speak to each other in hushed tones in an agitated manner and then they exit the stage. In a few moments a few more men enter the stage. They whisper to each other before exiting the stage. Vigorous gesturing and purposeful mannerisms suggest that the silhouetted figures are conspiring on something. Suddenly, the red background grows redder as something seems to be set on fire. Along with the flames fly ash and red hot sparks. Gradually, in the glow of fire, the two figures upon the plateau become clearer. They are dark and strong. One of them is aged beyond his prime, the other is younger—about thirty. They are bare bodied, cloth rolled up above their knees, sticks in hand—all sinews tensed in excitement.

Pradhan	(*Lifts his hand to indicate the red background.*) After all this is over, a day would come—my Shripati-Bhupati[85] had told me Kunja, believe me—that they would be welcomed like that. Beautiful like that, incomparable beauty like that. (*Laughs with sympathy and ridicule*) Three *morai*[86] of rice! Three heaps of rice, what are you saying Kunja! There is no peace till I give up my life. Kunja, O Kunja, I will kill myself. I will cheat the enemy by giving up my life. I will kill myself. My Shripati-Bhupati…

Clash of bamboo sticks within.

Kunja	(*Finger on his lips*) Silence. Make no sound. There…
Pradhan	Come, come Kunja, let's go ahead.
Kunja	What do you mean 'go ahead'—don't be mad!
Pradhan	Mad!
Kunja	You must be mad! (*Clash of bamboo sticks within*) Can you hear, there. There again.
Pradhan	What again? How many are they?
Kunja	How many? How can I say? Come away.
Pradhan	Come, let us go along the bank and surround them. Call them, Kunja.
Kunja	No, no, no, that can't be done… There again. Let us run from here.
Pradhan	Run! You want to run away?
Kunja	Aha! Aha! Is there a point in getting ourselves killed needlessly? Let us run into the woods.
Pradhan	(*Laments*) My heart is burning, Kunja! My soul is burning.

Kunja (*Pulls Pradhan by his hand*) You have made my life very difficult, do you get it, very difficult.

Enter Binodini with fearful steps.

Binodini (*As if in a trance*) O ma, I'm in trouble! Where should I go?

Enter Niranjan, terrorized.

Niranjan (*Running. Bare bodied*) Really, it is terrible!

Enter Panchanani.

Panchanani (*Walks quickly with the support of a stick*) No. Women can be safe no more. Women can't have any respect any more.

Exits quickly.

Enter Radhika. Her hair is loose as she runs across the stage frantically. Exit.

The twilight in the background has faded by now. Sound of conch shells being blown afar. A few figures swiftly run across the dark stage.

Enter Kunja.

Kunja (*Enters carefully, crouching*) It's all clear. They are gone. Come, come out all of you.

Enter Pradhan.

Pradhan (*Covers a wounded wrist with his hand*) Have they gone? But they will return again.

Kunja Is that blood? How did you get hurt? Show...

Pradhan (*Sneers*) Who cares for this blood? It has no

	value. To run and flee like wild animals in the forests—let it be Kunja. My soul is burning. My soul…
Kunja	Is there anyone whose soul isn't burnt? Mine is burnt too.
Pradhan	(*Angrily*) If it is burning why didn't you move forward when I asked you to? Why didn't you? Why did you refuse? If your soul…my Shripati-Bhupati…
Kunja	The pain of Shripati-Bhupati has not left me untouched, you know Jetha![87] But you seek some peace by uttering those names repeatedly. And I suffer in silence. That's the only difference. It's pointless, this lament.

Enter Panchanani.

Panchanani	(*Walks quickly with the support of a stick*) There has to be redressal of this, Kunja. Do you get it, there has to be redressal. Is this a way to work? Women will have to give up their honour and hide in the forest for hours! Why, why should this be? Aren't there any men left in this land, Kunja?
Kunja	Are you saying this, Jethima?[88]
Panchanani	Yes it's me. Why don't you answer me?
Kunja	What do you want me to do?
Panchanani	What is left for me to say? Can't you see, or have you turned a blind eye to everything? Should women suffer for you are weak? Have women committed any sin?
Kunja	What can I say?

Panchanani	What can you say?
Pradhan	You are supposed to tolerate all suffering. Bear it all in silence. Don't utter a word. To speak is sin. Silently...
Panchanani	What can you do? It's been three days since I have had a grain to eat. My body can take pain. That is nothing. But the disgrace... do women of this land have to give up their dignity? That which you always proclaim to be proud of! More importantly honour! The honour of women! Why are you mum? Why don't you say a thing? Come on, come on, Kunja, Kunja, Kunja!
Kunja	(*In rage*) Honour! Do you see any honour! Where life has lost all dignity, can women there have any honour? But...but...

Panchanani stares at Kunja for a few moments. Exit.

Pradhan	The 'but' has entered everyone. The very same 'but'. (*Suddenly he runs frantically and grabs Kunja by the throat*) I will take this 'but' by the throat (*desperately*). I will finish this 'but' off once and for all, finish it off forever. (*Struggles*)
Kunja	Jetha, Jetha, what's this, what are you doing? Jetha! Jetha!

Panchanani is thrown down as Kunja pushes.

Pradhan	(*Returning to his senses*) Yah!
Kunja	Jetha!
Pradhan	My soul is burning, Kunja, my soul is burning.

Pradhan gasps as he looks at Kunja.

Enter Judhisthir.

Judhisthir   Kunja!

Kunja   (*Notices Judhisthir*) You? When did you arrive?

Judhisthir   I've been here for nearly seven days.

Kunja   I did not get to know.

Judhisthir   True, you may not know but I've already come around twice. Three days ago, didn't a kabuliwallah visit this place of yours?

Kunja   (*Scratching his head*) Kabuliwallah? In the morning?

Judhisthir   Yes, around nine in the morning? (*Laughs*) I am that kabuliwallah.

Pradhan   You?

Judhisthir   You sat on a log smoking your hookah.

Kunja   Right!

Judhisthir   And another night. I was returning from Ratanganj on a horse. (*Kunja and Pradhan stare at Judhisthir in utter surprise*) Anyway. There is no need for you to know all of that. There isn't much time for that; I have to leave immediately. Just have a few urgent matters to tell you. From now on, we need to act tough against anyone who creates hurdles for us while we are carrying out our duties. There is no other way. We cannot afford to hesitate in doing any task towards the fulfilment of our objectives. No matter how cruel it may be. I am certain that victory will be ours, but it will not be easy, Kunja. We have to fight on, even if it means

	spilling blood, if we want to be victorious.
Pradhan	(*Lets out a vile laughter*) That is what I told Kunja, let us go forward, march ahead and surround them; but Kunja won't listen to me. Kunja always runs away. Only if my Shripati-Bhupati…
Kunja	(*To Judhisthir*) The loss of the two sons has really driven him insane.
Judhisthir	No, no. This is not insanity. This is what it should be. There is a need for this frenzy. This is not madness.
Pradhan	No. No.
Judhisthir	(*To Kunja*) You call this madness, but can you tell me Kunja, from where does this frenzy come? Why this madness? You are wrong, wrong Kunja. You are mistaken. Pradhan is not mad.
Kunja	Not mad.
Pradhan	(*Mumbles*) No, no, no, no.
Judhisthir	Our shortcomings can only be overcome by struggles within us.

Kunja is overcome with emotion. His eyes try to express his emotions but he is unable to say a word.

> (*Judhisthir pats Kunja on the back*) Kunja, my time is up. I will go now. (*To Pradhan*) I will come again, Pradhan.

As per the custom, Judhisthir touches his heart with his right hand and raises it above his head to say goodbye. Kunja and Pradhan imitate him.

Exit Judhisthir.

Suddenly, there is commotion within. The din grows gradually. Kunja looks around in great excitement. Pradhan also gets anxious. Clashing of bamboo sticks within.

Kunja Jetha! Jetha! There! (*He gestures asking Pradhan to follow him*)

Pradhan (*Laughing cruelly*) There, there again! O Kunja, Kunja, I will give up my life. I will give up my life! I will give up my life!

Exit quickly.

The commotion within has reached menacing proportions. In a few moments, the aged Panchanani enters, leading a crowd behind her.

Panchanani Go ahead all of you. March ahead!

The crowd advances while chanting 'Bande Mataram'.

March ahead all of you!

Clashing of bamboo sticks within! The crowd hesitates.

Come on go on, march ahead all of you.

Clashing of bamboo sticks within. The crowd stands still.

One Person (*Having been hit*) Arre baas re, baap re baap.

The crowd shrieks as it retreats.

Panchanani You are a disgrace to Aminpur, a blot on the face of Aminpur. That is why you have retreated. Don't retreat. March ahead. All of you move forward.

The crowd utters a raring sound and moves ahead.

Go ahead all of you...

Relentless sound of clashing bamboo sticks within. Panchanani falls on the ground holding her head.

>Go ahead, go ahead...

Panchanani is stupefied. Everyone moves across the plateau. A couple of figures fall on the ground wriggling in pain.

>(*Feebly*) Move ahead, go ahead all of you...

A couple of torches lie on the stage. The weapons are scattered all over. The din dies gradually.

Panchanani is no longer able to speak. She merely gestures—'Go ahead! Go ahead!'

Three to four figures lie on the stage and throw their limbs about wearily. Panchanani is unable to speak. Yet she continues to speak in gestures, 'Go ahead! Go ahead!' The din in the distance dies down. A couple of burning torches lie scattered on the stage.

Curtains

Scene Two

Pradhan's household. Unkempt. Pradhan, Kunja, Niranjan and Makhan sit on the verandah of a house with couple-roof. Radhika (aka Radhi) enters with an earthen pitcher full of water and goes into the house. A little later Radhika emerges from within the house with an old earthen pot and a sack. She places the pot on the ground and lays the sack on the porch. Then she takes paddy out of the pot and spreads them over the sack with her feet.

Radhi (*Spreading the paddy with her feet*) Here, these

	were the last resort. I had kept them away very carefully. Now all is finished.
Kunja	Why? What about the old aus[89] that I had kept away in the big black barrel on the roof?
Radhi	(*Rebuking*) Yes, that grain is still waiting for you up there. Do you have a clue of how many seers we need in a day?
Kunja	(*Annoyed*) No. I've never made that calculation. We've been surviving just like that.
Niranjan	(*Intervenes*) Come on now. Want and anguish are part of life. But there is no need for bitterness early in the morning. Don't fight.
Kunja	Just look at her behaviour. She could have told me clearly that the grains had finished. But no … I can't tolerate such language from women. It enrages me from head to toe. A total sloth but eats a lot, and look at her…
Radhi	Don't you see what a well-nourished body I have got? (*Makes a face*) Don't you utter one more word about the deeds of men. Even we women are ashamed of talking about it.
Kunja	O my bashful lady! (*Bites his tongue*)
Radhi	(*Sarcastically*) Too full for two eyes.

Exit Radhika.

Pradhan	(*Laments*) Ha! Rice! For two grains of rice…
Niranjan	(*Stops him*) All right, stop now. I don't want to hear anymore sobs from you. Your laments have wrecked my ears.
Kunja	Yes, having lost all is nothing but lament for us. Excellent affair.

Pradhan	(*Absentmindedly*) Was that a grain or two of rice? Three silos of paddy.
Kunja	(*To Niranjan*) There you go. Now do what you will!

Pradhan lets off a huge sigh.

Niranjan	(*To Pradhan*) You had time to think before you destroyed it.[90]
Kunja	Think? Not only did he destroy his own stock, he actually convinced several others to destroy their own storage.
Pradhan	Pradhan did not force anyone to destroy their grains.
Niranjan	Have I claimed that you have destroyed other people's silos of rice? You persuaded them to do so. What can't be done using persuasion.
Pradhan	I did not persuade anyone.
Kunja	Okay, you did not persuade anyone. But you demonstrated your plans to them.
Pradhan	Yes, I did demonstrate.
Niranjan	Were you aware of what you were doing?
Pradhan	(*Angry*) Yes, yes I was aware. Do whatever you can. I have held back the boat.[91] With a day's notice I have driven all people from their land. I have done everything. Do unto me what you will!

He is agitated.

Kunja	(*Gestures to Niranjan asking him to be silent*) Who wants to do anything to you? It is when you start lamenting that these matters come up.

Nabanna ▪ 43

	Those who have gone, have gone. In just a few months there will be a fresh crop of rice. If nothing untoward occurs there will be no want of grain. (*To Radhika*) Why? Where did you go? (*To Makhan*) Go Makhan, call your Ma.
Makhan	What will Ma do?
Kunja	(*Chiding him*) What she does is my headache. Call her right now, you impudent fellow!
Makhan	Going, I'm going.

Exit Makhan.

Kunja	He was weaned just the other day and look at him shoot off his mouth. It is all his mother's doing.

Enter Radhika.

	You went off in a temper. But everyone will be unfed if you are in a tiff.
Radhi	O, ma! When was I in a tiff?
Kunja	You stamped off into the room, which made me think you were cross.
Radhi	So what if I stamped my feet. It doesn't seem to bother anyone.
Kunja	It does bother. Of course it does. I am not sitting idle. Come on now, give me that thing of yours, that…
Radhi	(*Angry as she tries to guess*) Give what?
Kunja	(*With eyes closed*) Arre! What is it called?
Radhi	Aha! Aha! This buffoonery makes me want to hang myself!
Kunja	Ah! Yes! I remember now. Your…

Radhi	Anklets, isn't it?
Kunja	Yes.
Radhi	Did I not realize that! You remembered it all the while, you put on a false appearance of amnesia as you are ashamed to ask for it. It is a gift from my parents. My mother gave me those anklets. I have kept them away. I will not give them to you. You have gobbled up everything else. Now you've laid your eyes upon the anklets. Destiny!
Kunja	Don't give if you don't want to. Don't keep chanting 'Destiny! Destiny!' Kunja Samaddar still breathes! He isn't dead! Not yet!
Radhi	Great! Let him prove that! I would be fortunate.
Kunja	Of course! You thought my death would make it easy for you to eat and sleep in peace. Stop daydreaming! That's not happening!

He rushes into the room and pulls out a whole lot of utensils.

> She never tires reminding that her parents are rich. I don't care for your arrogance and taunts.

He drops the utensils with a clang. Radhika walks off quickly.

Niranjan	Where are you taking those to?
Kunja	To the shop, where else? We need to fill the stomachs of the entire clan!

He exits into the house coughing and murmuring.

Pradhan	Makhan! O Makhan!
Niranjan	To hell with your family. Bastard! I'll leave today itself!

Enter Binodini with a pitcher.

Binodini Where will you go?

Niranjan Here comes another clown. The entire lot is here.

Binodini O, ma! What have I done?

Niranjan Nothing! You've done nothing! Now go away, I can't take it any more. Bastard, I'll leave today for sure!

Binodini Where will you go?

Niranjan Have I decided where to go? I shall go wherever these two feet take me.

Binodini O, ma! What are you saying?

Niranjan What else! My ears are cooked with the constant bickering in this family. I will leave today.

Binodini You must take me with you.

Niranjan (*Grimacing*) Take me with you! Where will you go? Where will you go? I don't even have a place of my own, and, wait a while, let me go! I'll try to get some kind of a job, then I'll think about it.

Binodini You'll go alone?

Niranjan (*Grimacing*) Where will I get a companion from?

Binodini Why? Take me with you?

Niranjan Have you lost your mind? I have no idea of where I'll go. Don't bother me needlessly, let me be.

Binodini But you aren't leaving today?

Niranjan If I want to go today, what's stopping me? What's holding me back?

Binodini	If you want to be held back, there is enough reason for that. I'll be left here, all alone.
Niranjan	Why should you be alone? Women are always whining.
Binodini	What can I do if I was born a woman?
Niranjan	Good you did. Now don't crib. There are other people here. You'll have to live with them. If you manage, well and good, if you don't, there's little that I can do. I have to go.

Binodini wipes her tears.

> I am not leaving you to fend for yourself. Dada, Boudi, Jetha, Makhan—all are here. What is there to be afraid of? None of them is a stranger. You can see for yourself the conditions. It is getting impossible to make ends meet. If I sit around doing nothing, can you imagine what may happen tomorrow? Mere whining won't do any good. You need to judge the circumstances. (*With a heavy voice*) I too can cry like that. But what are tears worth? Nothing at all!

Enter Kunja, tired.

Kunja   (*Addressing Niranjan*) You hit her again? (*Niranjan doesn't answer*) Again you've hit this woman?

Exit Binodini in tears.

> (*Shouts*) Get out, get out of my house immediately. Rascal! Chamar! Want has knocked your senses off you. Get out right now! You beast!

In a state of rage he picks up a log of wood and hits Niranjan on the head.

> You dare to hit a woman... get out, get out I say!

Niranjan bleeds from his head. Exit.

> (*In shock*) Ha! Blood! Blood! I have killed him! I have murdered Niranjan! Niranjan! Niranjan!

Curtains

Scene Three

Pradhan sits on the porch outside the room smoking his hookah. Kunja stands in the courtyard digging mud with his toes. They are in the middle of a discussion.

Pradhan	(*Takes a long draw from his hookah and lets off the smoke*) Should I let it be? I don't know what you are saying?
Kunja	What can I say? It is your land, you decide what you want to do!
Pradhan	That I will, but what do you say?
Kunja	I have said what I had to say.
Pradhan	What is that?
Kunja	There is no point selling it—you sold off the Mogra land. How long did the money last? So what's the use of selling off the land at a throwaway price? What's done is done. No need to sell any more. Ah! And all you have is three bighas of land.

Pradhan	All right, then tell me clearly what I should do.
Kunja	You need more clarity? I am telling you not to sell the land. You have already sowed the grain. Poverty has always been there. It will remain whether you sell the land or not. Let us wait and see. Things can't be the same forever.

Enter Dayal.

Dayal	(*Clears his throat, addresses Pradhan*) O Pradhan! I see you are at home!
Pradhan	(*Looks around*) Yes, it has been overcast since the morning.
Dayal	It may rain.
Pradhan	Sit down. Have a smoke.
Dayal	How can I have a smoke? (*Sits down*)
Pradhan	Why? Are you going somewhere?
Dayal	No just…
Pradhan	(*Gives the hookah to Dayal*) Take this.
Kunja	(*Sitting at one end of the courtyard*) Dayalda, what do you say about this matter?
Dayal	Which matter?
Pradhan	O, it's nothing.
Dayal	Still, let me hear.
Kunja	Jetha has three bighas of farmland beside the marsh. He wants to sell it off.
Dayal	So?
Kunja	I suggested that sorrows and hardships are there. There is no real gain in selling the small piece of land.
Dayal	That is correct. You may be able to get some money from the sale of land, but without any

	regular source of livelihood it won't last long. I have committed this mistake.
Kunja	What? Have you sold your land?
Dayal	Yes, at least a part of it. But what difference did it make? I failed to save even the seed grain. Oh!
Kunja	Oh I see! You are in even deeper trouble. You have lost all you had!
Dayal	All, Kunja. Everything. Or else would Dayalda have had to beg from door to door for a fistful of rice?
Pradhan	Do you understand Dayal, there may be pardon for small errors, but there are no excuses for big mistakes. You'll have to atone for them.
Kunja	(*With a sigh*) You did learn (*to Dayal*), but too late.
Dayal	(*With a sorry chuckle*) It was so late that there was no way of undoing it.
Pradhan	(*Takes the hookah from Dayal*) Then let the land be.
Dayal	Yes, let the asset be. One should not sell off property; moreover…
Pradhan	You say that, but how will we make ends meet? One has to survive.
Dayal	Are you in the same boat?
Pradhan	What else were you thinking?
Dayal	Why, you did have some rice, didn't you, Pradhan?
Pradhan	That was on another day. Today, there is nothing!
Dayal	Oh! Is that the state? I thought let me visit Pradhan and ask him if he could…

Pradhan	Huh! What can I say about it! Just this morning after a lot of bickering and bloodshed, Kunja went off to sell the last couple of copper vessels we had. He's returned with about two seers of rice. Imagine! We are a family of five. Who do we feed?
Dayal	True! But what will I do. There hasn't been a grain of rice at home for two days now. Ranga's mother has been almost gasping for breath since last evening. What should I do?
Kunja	What else? This is what it has come to.
Dayal	Kunja!
Kunja	What more can I say? Ranga's mother has been gasping for breath since yesterday afternoon, someone else has been gasping for breath since yesterday, another person has been gasping for breath since this morning—this is all we will hear from now on. (*Gets a bit of rice from the room, wrapped in his dhoti*) Here, take this. But, Dayalda, I won't be able to give you more than a fistful. This is the last we have.
Dayal	(*Spreads out his dhoti for the rice*) This is enough. At least it will save our lives.
Kunja	But for how long will we carry on like this?
Dayal	As long as we can. As long as there is life, there is hope.
Pradhan	Hope alone will not feed us, Dayal. We'll have to do something about it.
Dayal	Tell me what is to be done. I am with you.
Pradhan	Let us go to the city. The babus have set up relief camps.

Nabanna ▪ 51

Kunja	Don't utter a word about the babus.
Dayal	Yes, let us not speak of the babus.
Kunja	They are merely engaged in an eyewash.
Pradhan	Are you abusing the bhadraloks? But the bhadraloks are our only resort right now. Do what you will, but you'll have to seek help from the bhadralok.
Kunja	What makes a bhadralok? Just because someone puts on clean clothes and struts about mouthing chaste bangla, we don't have to do as they say. Chhi!
Pradhan	Why should we do that?
Kunja	Then?
Dayal	Let that be. What's happened has happened. Tell us what we should do now.
Pradhan	That is what I've been trying to tell you. I say…
Kunja	What is there to be said? Our condition is the same as scores of others. We too will have to hit the streets like scores of others.
Pradhan	So it's finally happened! What I've been fearing all along has finally happened.
Dayal	There is nothing left to happen. There is only one road before us. We all have to take the same route.
Pradhan	That is why I say, let's go to the city.
Kunja	It makes little difference whether we go to the city or to hell! We have to beg around in the streets, that is all.
Pradhan	Beg on the streets, Dayal. Pradhan Samaddar will have to beg on the streets.
Dayal	This is what it has come to. We had to see this

	day. Destiny! Destiny!
Pradhan	Why else would I have lost all my land, and why else would I have had to step out onto the streets. It is nothing but destiny.
Kunja	Don't blame destiny for everything. If you've chosen to play with fire, you'll get burnt. Don't blame destiny for it. I swear Dayalda, I can never understand what you say. You are…

Makhan storms in.

Makhan	Get onto the roof, all of you! Get onto the roof. A huge wave is coming our way—it is very high, seven or eight feet high. Hoo! Hoo!

Sound of storm within.

Kunja	He is right!

Exit Makhan; moves into the room.

Dayal	Pradhan, I'll go now. It has been overcast since morning, there's hot air blowing since last night. What's the matter?

A gust of wind.

Arre-b-baas!

Exit Dayal.

Kunja	Sit down, Dayalda. Don't go out under such conditions.

Another gust of wind. Sound of the breaking of a large tree. Pradhan gets off the porch onto the courtyard. He places his hand over his eyebrows trying to look out for the wave. His hair is dancing in the wind. Green leaves, twigs, branches, etc. fly into the courtyard. The couple-roof shakes repeatedly such that it seems that it may fall off at any moment. The blizzard continues to wreck havoc. The light dims. A little later painful cries of the helpless can be heard. Possibly someone is trapped. Such sounds seem to come in far and across the village. Soon the roof of Pradhan's house falls off.[92]

Pradhan (*Almost insane amidst the chaos*) Kunja! Makhan! (*Wipes the water off his face and eyes*) Makhan, this way! Kunja! Makhan!

Enter Makhan, anxious.

Makhan Here Dadu! I am here! Where is Baba? Baba!

Enter Radhika.

Radhika (*Runs in*) Makhan! Makhan! Where's Makhan? Makhan!
Makhan I'm here! Right here!
Radhika Where! (*Embraces Makhan*) My darling!
Pradhan Where's Kunja? Kunja!
Kunja (*Voice unclear*) Here! Makhan! Here!
Pradhan Where? Kunja! Makhan, where is your father?
Makhan Dadu, he's here! Dadu! Raise the roof. He is trapped under it. Hold it, hold it, raise it!

Pradhan runs up and raises the roof. Radhika helps Kunja out.

Radhika Are you hurt?
Kunja No. Where's Makhan? Here he is.
Pradhan Is everyone else all right?
Radhika (*Anxiously*) Where's Bino?
Kunja Go have a look! Come on quick! Look for her! Is she trapped in there? There…

Makhan Here, Baba, here!

Everyone advances towards Binodini. Binodini is unconscious. Radhika bends over Binodini.

Radhika O ma!... Look here all of you! O Bino, Bino!

Kunja, Radhika and Makhan carry Binodini out and lay her down in the open space in front.

Kunja (*Lifts Binodini's eyelids*) She must be hurt real bad.

Radhika B-i-n-o! O, B-i-n-o!

Binodini groans.

Pradhan Is she alive, Kunja?

Kunja A-ha! Will you keep quiet!

Radhika (*Gently brushes her hand over Binodini's head*) Don't utter such evil words. O Bino, Bino. A little... what? Where have you been hurt?

Kunja Let her be. Don't disturb her.

Cries of distress within.

Pradhan Just the house was left for shelter. Now that is gone as well. The street could not wait for us to step into it, Kunja. The paths have entered our home. Our home is now lost. O Kunja, what you said has been proved right, what you said is true. Pradhan Samaddar is on the streets today. Kunja—didn't you say...

Cries of 'Kunja! Kunja!' within.

Kunja (*Tries to hear*) Ha... Kunja! Who's there?

Enter Dayal, in a state of frenzy.

Kunja	Dayalda! What's happened Dayalda?
Dayal	(*Takes out the rice from the folds of his cloth and holds it out*) Here is the rice that you gave, Kunja! The rice that you gave!
Kunja	(*Surprised*) Dayalda! Dayalda!
Dayal	(*As if in a trance*) Ha! Did I ever have anything of my own! Was there anyone I called my own? Was there anyone? Where are they? I never had anyone.
Kunja	You took the rice for Ranga's mother…
Dayal	Ranga's mother! Where is Ranga's mother? Where is Ranga? Where is my house? My home! Kunja!
Pradhan	Dayal!
Dayal	It is the sea all over, Pradhan, the sea is all over. Only water all around and there is nothing else… The sea has swallowed the village. Ranga's mother, Ranga's mother, Ranga's mother! Ranga's mother!

Sound of the storm.

Curtains

Scene Four

A dilapidated home and its surroundings. The roof is falling off. The thatch is missing at a few places, the framework is visible. The state of poverty is apparent from the faces of the members of the family.

Binodini sits at a mud stove in the courtyard trying to boil something in a handi. A sick Makhan is present on the porch.

Binodini (*Tries to blow into the fire. But the smoke gets into her eyes. She rubs her eyes.*) Baabba! Can these green leaves ever burn? The smoke will turn me blind. I can't sit here anymore.

Makhan Why the hell are you sitting there! Just place a thick branch there and come and sit here on the porch. It's nothing but wild figs boiling in there—even cows don't eat such things. Put a branch there and move away. There's nothing much to be cooked.

Binodini Don't you just sit there like a wisecrack, Makhan. Shut up! Be grateful for this cooking, and…

Makhan Same thing everyday—boiled wild figs and tubers. I won't have them today…

Binodini Don't eat. It's your choice. I don't care. Why don't you go and get some delicacies for yourself.

Enter Pradhan. He looks tired. His feet are covered with mud. He has got a bunch of crabs with him.

Pradhan (*With a smile*) Is getting hold of delicacies any easy task? (*Shaking the crabs*) I managed to get these with great difficulty. Come on, get a vessel. Na, where will you get one…something to put these in.

Binodini gets up.

Just get anything. Oof! It is itching all over. Old, smelly mud.

Exit Binodini.

Makhan Where did you catch them? Quite a few of them. The ones you had got the other day were tiny. These are quite large.

Pradhan (*Smiles*) They have grown. The water is drying up. They are moving on to the streams. It's not easy catching them.

Enter Binodini with a broken basket.

Good, you've got it. Keep it here. (*With a laugh*) Fry it nicely with salt and chilli...and let Makhan have two of them.

Enter Kunja.

Kunja What will you give to Makhan? Don't give him anything to eat. Jitenbabu has advised not to give him any such thing to eat. He repeated it many times.

Makhan No, no I won't eat. I will just taste a bit.

Kunja Forget those luxuries! 'I will just taste!' Taste what? What is this stuff?

Makhan Crabs.

Kunja What? Crabs? You'll have crabs? Make sure you do not give him crabs and such stuff. I am making it clear to everyone.

Pradhan Why are you scolding everyone for this? He always has a temper.

Enter Radhika with a bunch of herbs.

Kunja   (*In anger and disgust*) Temper! You can only see my temper. You see temper in this? I spent the entire afternoon going all over in the hot sun and brought back a little bit of broken rice as the doctor had said. And what do I find? The boy is nagging for crabs! To hell with love and care. (*Throws away the broken rice from his gamchha*[93]) Let it be, there is no need for the rice anymore.

Radhika   Why did you take all the trouble to get the broken rice? And then let it all go waste?

Kunja   (*Anguished*) I have never got anything in return for any trouble I have ever taken. My efforts have never been considered of any worth.

Radhi looks on with eyes full of pity.

Pradhan   (*Gets up*) Just look at what he has done! (*He tries to gather the rice grains together with his hands*) He toiled the entire day to find these grains, and just because I uttered something, he threw them away.

Kunja   Any trouble, if at all, has been mine to take. No one else needs to care for it.

Pradhan   (*Gathering the rice*) If you could feel the pain, then I would have no sorrows!

Kunja   Let it be. There is no need for your false tears. Enough! All pretence!

Pradhan   (*With a vacant stare*) What was that? What did you say, Kunja? Pretence? False tears? My compassion appears false to you? You've insulted me. You insulted me? You've insulted me...

Pradhan cries.

Kunja It always comes upon me. It always does. When did I insult you?

Pradhan Was it not an insult? How else do you want to insult me? What else do you want to do to me? For you, all my sorrow and compassion is nothing but a show! Instead of saying all that why don't you hit my head with...

He picks up a log of wood and hits himself on the head. Radhika shrieks.

Kunja (*Runs and holds Pradhan's hands*) What is this, Jetha? What are you doing?

Pradhan (*Agitated*) Kill me Kunja. Put an end to all my pain. It will end my pain.

He groans.

Kunja (*Throws down the log*) Chhi! Chhi! Chhi! Chhi! You don't even know what you've just said in the heat of the moment! You're becoming juvenile day by day! All I had said was that since Makhan is not well, the doctor had advised that he not be fed things like crabs. Was there really a need to create such a ruckus for this? Chhi! Chhi! Chhi! Chhi!

Pradhan Sick! Really! What illness does he have?

Kunja His limbs have swollen up, his eyes are yellowish. Isn't he ill?

Pradhan Understood. But is he sick because of food or

	because of lack of food? Did you find out?

Kunja remains silent.

Radhika	He has been starving for almost a month now. How much does he get to eat?
Kunja	What do people eat when they are sick?
Pradhan	Sick! Sick! Ha! Sick! Kunja, I will never be able to forget that the boy is just starving to death, little by little, just for want of food.
Kunja	No, no, he is very ill. Jetha, the doctor has told us he is suffering from a dreaded disease. Jetha, you just don't know.
Makhan	I am hungry. I want to eat something. Please give me something to eat, I want to eat.
Pradhan	I can never accept, I can never forget that just for want of food...
Kunja	Jetha, he is very sick. You are mistaken. He has a dreaded disease.
Pradhan	I will never forget that the boy just starved to death. No one can make me forget that.

Curtains

Scene Five

Same scene. Life is on death bed due to an epic famine. Cries of 'Bolo Hari! Hari Bol!'[94] and 'Maago'[95] within. Constant sounds of groaning and agonized shrieks. Radhika is ill. She sits on the porch near the sick Makhan. Her hair is dishevelled. Binodini is sweeping the courtyard with a broom.

Binodini (*Leaning towards Radhika*) Ofh! This sound is unending. It has been ringing in my ears all day! Uhh! So many people are dying!

Radhika Is anything left of it! The entire village is devastated. In Uttarpara everyone is suffering from—no, let me not name it. It is all over. The situation is so bad that there is no one to put some water in another person's mouth. I don't know what will be the end of this. I have never seen such a famine. I have never seen such death.

Binodini (*Sits down*) There was a famine like this many years ago. Of course, none of us saw it. I heard my mother speak of it. Even she hadn't seen it. She heard of it from my grandmother. Do you know about it, Didi?

Radhika No.

Binodini (*Stands up*) It seems it was worse than this one.

She resumes sweeping the floor. Radhika shakes her head with a soft sound of denial. Haru Dutta clears his throat within.

Haru Dutta (*Within*) Ye, Pradhan?

Enter Haru Dutta.

Ye-e-e, Pradhan, are you in?

Having seen Haru Dutta, Binodini covers her head with her anchal[96] and turns around. Radhika covers her head.

Radhika He's not at home.

Haru Dutta	Arre! Here, Makhan's mother, but Pradhan just told me...
Radhika	(*Lays down a sac on the porch*) He's asked you to wait.
Haru Dutta	He has asked me to wait?
Radhika	Yes, he said, 'I'll be back soon. Ask him to wait if he comes.'
Haru Dutta	Will he come back soon?
Radhika	That is what he said.
Haru Dutta	(*Sits down*) He left and asked me to wait. Uh, who's lying there?
Radhika	That is Makhan. It has been several days, he hasn't spoken a word. His face is all swollen. I don't know what lies in store.
Haru Dutta	O! Are you unwell too? Your face seems to have paled.
Radhika	(*Touches her forehead*) I have had fever for the last few days. It has not eased.
Haru Dutta	O! So are you taking any medicine?
Radhika	(*In a sorry tone*) Where will we get any medicine? One tablet costs...
Haru Dutta	The bark of the neem tree. I don't mean anything else. Just the bark of the neem tree. Wash it well in an earthen pot...no, you won't be able to manage it. There are a few processes. You can send someone over with a small bottle.
Radhika	(*To Binodini*) Why are you standing facing the other way? You should not be shy before someone your father's age. Come, sit here.
Haru Dutta	(*Laughs*) Who's that? Niranjan's wife? Just look

	at this. I thought it was someone else. Achha! Everyday we meet several times on the street, yet she is so bashful. Hehe! But that's good, modesty. After all she is a daughter-in-law. That's good.
Radhika	(*With a sidelong glance at Binodini*) She is like that, but you have not seen. (*She grimaces at Binodini and tries to show Haru Dutta that Binodini is talkative*) Why are you still standing like an oiled bamboo? Come and sit here. The gentleman is like your father.

Binodini's eyes flash wide open. After a moment's hesitation she walks off.

	(*Insinuation directed towards Binodini*) Did you see!
Haru Dutta	Hehe! She is immature. Anyway do send a bottle with someone. It's not good to carry on with fever. Times are not good, not good. You can see all around.
Radhika	Have I not noticed. My blood curdles in fear!
Haru Dutta	(*Raising his eyebrows*) Uuu…

Enter Pradhan.

	Here you are.
Pradhan	(*A little baffled*) Oh, I got a bit late. Have you been here long?
Haru Dutta	Yes, it's been a while. I've been waiting for you.
Pradhan	(*Scratches his head*) Oh really…I had asked you to wait.
Haru Dutta	Yes, I heard that. And what have you decided?

Pradhan	Maane? What should I say?
Haru Dutta	What does that mean? (*Raises his hand*) Just let me know if you will sell it. Tell me what's in your mind. I'm not forcing you to sell your land.
Pradhan	Then wait for a while, let Kunja return.
Haru Dutta	Kunja will come?
Pradhan	Kunja will be back any moment.
Haru Dutta	But what do I need Kunja for. I have nothing to do with him. And if you want to discuss the matter with him, haven't you done so already?
Pradhan	Discussion? There's nothing much. But I did talk to him.
Haru Dutta	You spoke to him?
Pradhan	Yes, I told him, since land is...
Haru Dutta	Let that be, what you discussed with him is none of my business. So, what did Kunja have to say?
Pradhan	He said...
Haru Dutta	Tell me...
Pradhan	He is advising against it. He says there is no point selling the land at this price.
Haru Dutta	Against it! O! O! O! So what is your opinion?
Pradhan	Me-e-e! I s-a-y, you know what...
Haru Dutta	Pradhan, this is not the first time that I am dealing with you. You know me very well, isn't it? You judge it for yourself. Just the other day I purchased the Mogra marshland. Now just check what others have paid for that kind of land, and what I have paid you. In a way if I

buy this land from you it will be a loss for me. I won't be able to make any cash by selling it. You can say it is residential land, but right now it is uninhabited. And I am not about to start cultivation. It will stay as is. I'd just be blocking a fair bit of money in this. What more do you expect me to do. There are all these charities that are distributing rice, dal, feeding khichdi, distributing clothes. To tell you the truth, I am also doing this as a charity—giving cash in exchange for mud. Does land have any value today? Anyway, it is your goat. You decide whether to cut at the head or at its tail. But I will not be able to pay any greater price for the land. You need to think twice before you suggest the impossible.

Enter Kunja. He carries a stack of grass on his head.

	Oh! Kunja, you are here. Where did you get the grass from?
Kunja	From all around.
Haru Dutta	O! This grass seems to be from my land at Dholkalmi. You've taken whatever you have. Now don't take any more. Grass prices are very high these days.
Kunja	I've just taken two bundles.
Haru Dutta	Yes, those two bunches would fetch about eight paise. Don't take any more. So, Pradhan, what have we decided? Will you have time tomorrow?
Kunja	(*Looking with a slant at Haru Dutta he speaks to*

	Pradhan) What is this all about? The sale of the land?
Haru Dutta	(*Laughs*) Imagine what he is saying? Fine, I will let you take more grass. Does anything else grow these days? Huh! You take your grass.
Kunja	Whatever you may say, the land is not up for sale.
Haru Dutta	What will you eat? You can't satisfy your hunger with the soil! 'Land is not up for sale!'
Kunja	Saying all that won't help.
Haru Dutta	(*Laughs*) You shut up! You are a child. What do you understand of land. All right then, Pradhan, we will settle it tomorrow.
Kunja	Jetha won't settle anything. I am telling you that this land will not be sold. You seem be hanging onto Jetha like a leech. This land is not for sale.
Haru Dutta	Heh! Heh! Heh! Pradhan, your nephew is a fool, he doesn't know a thing. I got to know that Makhan's mother is suffering from fever. What harm will it do (to Kunja) to come over to my place and get a bit of the panchan?[97] You must come, or send someone to come and get it.
Kunja	The real illness is starvation. Medicines are of no use.
Haru Dutta	Starvation! Pradhan, your nephew is funny. He can make up stories. Anyway, then as we decided, let's settle it tomorrow.

Prepares to exit.

| **Pradhan** | No. I will not sell the land. I have lost |

	everything, I won't sell the land.
Haru Dutta	Fine, you take the full amount from me.
Pradhan	No, let it be.
Haru Dutta	What do you mean, 'Let it be'? You take from me whatever price you want.
Pradhan	Kunja!
Kunja	In the past you have used the lure of money to buy off all grains from the village. Now you are trying to seize land. Tell him the land will not be sold.
Pradhan	Yes, that is what I'll tell him—I will not sell. Let it be.
Haru Dutta	Pradhan, you've given me your word. Don't go back on it now.
Kunja	What 'giving of a word' are you talking about? Who made any promise to you? You are torturing the poor. He who owns the land says that he won't sell it, and he says that it is a breach of promise? What a great keeper of promises!
Pradhan	(*Tries to stop Kunja*) Aha! Kunja, you keep quiet.
Kunja	(*Shouting*) Why should I keep quiet? You want to keep quiet? If you continue to tolerate everything quietly, you will turn dumb one day.
Pradhan	I want to be dumb, you keep quiet.
Kunja	Why, for what? Shout out now. Call everyone. Expose this man now.
Pradhan	Aha, I am telling you to keep quiet.
Kunja	Keep quiet!

Haru Dutta	The fellow is talking too much!
Kunja	You still fear him, you still fear him!
Haru Dutta	If he doesn't fear me, at least...

Points upwards.

Kunja	I know you will point upwards. I have lost that fear too. I don't have faith anymore.
Haru Dutta	Oh! So you have a taut backbone, I see. It needs a bit of bending. You uncivilized brute, you have crossed your limit.
Kunja	Ei! Don't abuse me. Be careful.

Haru Dutta's younger daughter, Mati, enters in a hurry.

Haru Dutta	(*Holds his daughter back*) Is 'uncivilized' an abusive word? Just check out this son of a bitch! Is 'uncivilized' an abuse?
Kunja	Hold your tongue. Be careful of what you say.
Haru Dutta	Just look at his audacity! Just look...
Mati	Baba!
Haru Dutta	Go Mati! Call your Mama! And everyone else who is at the Chandimandap. Go!

Exit Mati, hastily.

Pradhan	You should go now. There is just one piece of land. And I won't sell it. It's over.
Haru Dutta	It's not over, not yet. I won't let it be over so easily.
Pradhan	You are needlessly dragging the matter, Babu.
Haru Dutta	I am dragging the matter. O! You may be aged, but you are quite a scoundrel.

Kunja (*Boasts*) Go on! Do what you will! Who cares for your threats?

Kunja exits in a hurry.

Enter two–three able-bodied men with sticks.

Haru Dutta Give him a few good blows.

Enter Kunja with a stick. Kunja is hit.

First Man (*To Kunja*) Rascal! He is starving. And yet he is acting smart.

Second Man Ei! Touch his feet and beg forgiveness!

Kunja crawls up to Haru Dutta. The latter drags away his feet as he bites his tongue.

Haru Dutta Don't touch my feet! Don't touch my feet! Yuck!

Enter Binodini. Hearing the commotion, Makhan, unwell and lying in the verandah, tries to stand up but falls onto the ground. Radhika and Binodini cry out.

Hitting Kunja in the face with a stick.

You impudent rascal! How dare you speak up! (*Hits the ground with the stick*) Don't you know who you are talking to? Don't you know?

Kunja, insulted and in pain, cries like a child.

Pradhan Don't kill him! Ore baba! Baba, please don't kill him, don't kill him.

Second Man You! (*Beats Pradhan with a stick. Pradhan falls down*)

Kunja's cries grow louder. Makhan tries to gather all his strength and stands up, but he swoons and falls again. Binodini, Radhika and Pradhan rush to him. All of them bend over a dying Makhan.

Radhika   Hai! Hai! Hai! Hai! I have lost everything! O Makhan! Makhan!
Pradhan   (*To Binodini*) Get a bit of water. Water...
Radhika   O Makhon! Makhon!

Makhan groans in pain.

Pradhan   Makhan, Makhan re! K-k-Kunja, look at Makhan once! Just once!

Radhika cries profusely. Binodini looks on with a fearful face. A gloom seems to descend on her.

Kunja   (*Raises his head*) Ya! Makhan! Makhan...
Pradhan   You left us Makhan!

Curtains

Act Two

Scene One

Kalidhan's shop. Kalidhan leans on a thick bolster on a high platform at one corner. He is dark, fat, well fed, wears a loose muslin shirt, a gold chain around his neck, an amulet on his arm. Above his head is an idol of Ganesh. On the wall beneath the idol is a ritual mark in vermilion and is inscribed with the following: 'This business operates by the grace of Shri Shri Kalimata.' Beside him, wrapped in red cloth, lies a heap of notebooks. In the middle of the room stands a huge pair of scales. Scattered around it lie weights of various measures—large and small. A few empty bags are kept on one side of the godown. A coolie and the manager are walking about. In front of them coolies carry heavy sacks of rice into a hidden chamber of the godown. Kalidhan, bent over the cash-box, is busy in calculations. Now and again he mutters something to himself. Haru Dutta sits cross-legged smartly at one end of the platform. He looks up at Kalidhan repeatedly as he smokes a bidi. From the looks of the two, it seems like some calculations are being made and some strategy is being devised. The young manager Niranjan (aka Rakhahari), walks up to Kalidhan while jiggling with a bunch of keys.

Niranjan	All goods have been put in the godown.
Kalidhan	Has all of it been loaded properly?
Niranjan	Yes, it…
Kalidhan	All of it…

He points to the secret chamber.

Niranjan	In the third chamber.
Kalidhan	Third chamber! All right. Now you go there. Go! Go! (*Returns to the calculations*) The keys…
Niranjan	Yes, let me lock the chamber.
Kalidhan	You haven't locked it yet! How many times do I have to tell you? Nah! I'll have to wind up my business.

Niranjan moves to exit.

> Listen. Don't be in such a hurry to go. Listen to me carefully. Pull the lock several times to make sure it has been locked properly. And before coming back, station two bags into the hole. Have you understood? Go!

Exit Niranjan.

> You should be careful at all times. Is it possible to repeat these instructions time and again? Go, finish the task quickly. (*He addresses Haru Dutta but intends the words for Niranjan*) I have to run my business with the help of such people. He is a good for nothing, just bull dung. (*Lowers his voice*) I have kept him simply because he is trustworthy. He won't spill a word even if he is tortured.

Haru Dutta	That's a great merit.
Kalidhan	That's why I have kept him.
Haru Dutta	It is very difficult to find reliable people these days.
Kalidhan	(*Raises his eyebrows*) True. (*He gets back to the calculations, mumbling.*) So we have... No, wait a bit. Wait for Ramhari. Arre... (*Goes back to calculations*) have a bidi.
Haru Dutta	Yes, yes. (*Smokes*) But I have to go for some work.
Kalidhan	Take this. (*Hands him the matches. After some more calculations.*) Dutta, the rice you've got this year is not very good.
Haru Dutta	It is good. In a few days there won't be any rice, and you... Conditions have become very bad in the suburbs. People are almost killing each other.

Stares at Kalidhan.

Kalidhan	Fine, but the fellow who supplies rice to the Nandis, where is he able to source such quality from? You won't find any flaw in it—no broken grain or anything.
Haru Dutta	Yes I know. But did you find out the rate?
Kalidhan	How much?
Haru Dutta	Twenty-two and a half. Will you pay that much? Will you?
Kalidhan	Twenty-two and a half!
Haru Dutta	What else? Can it go higher than that?
Kalidhan	Twenty-two and a half is too much.
Haru Dutta	You'll have to pay for quality. There can be no

	other way. If you want I can try to get a few boatfuls. But that would be the price—twenty-two and a half, twenty-three, nothing less. If you want some, let me know.
Kalidhan	No. I won't be able to pay such high prices. It would be a complete loss for me.
Haru Dutta	Where is the loss? Customers will grab them for thirty or forty. Are the Nandis making a loss?
Kalidhan	Let the Nandis do what they want. I won't be able to match their price. No one can predict the market, Dutta. It is behaving like a weathercock. Ore baap re…
Haru Dutta	(*Faking laughter*) See now. If this is what you say, what would be the state of other traders?
Kalidhan	Don't you understand, Dutta? I've got at least a lakh and a quarter of goods stashed away at various places. If I don't manage to recover this I would be hit.
Haru Dutta	You will recover them for sure.
Kalidhan	That is easy for you to say. But till the recovery happens I'm unable to sleep at night, Dutta. All kinds of thoughts keep swarming around me like nightmares.
Haru Dutta	I think you should get your blood pressure checked. Big people should have sophisticated ailments and you've got yours.
Kalidhan	You said it.

Enter Niranjan.

Finally, you've come!

Haru Dutta	Good! Now please hurry up. I'm getting late.
Kalidhan	I won't be paying the entire amount today.
Haru Dutta	What? Why? All right then, pay what you will. I have to go.
Kalidhan	(*Laughs*) Oh! Are you visiting the Guin's? I didn't manage to catch up on that gossip. You always seem to be in such a hurry that it is impossible to gather any sort of news from you. If you sit down for a moment or two we may be able to discuss the state of the market. (*To Niranjan*) How many bags did you say?
Niranjan	Altogether, twenty-seven.
Kalidhan	Twenty-seven bags. Now one cart of...
Haru Dutta	Please give me the money and then go on with your calculations.
Kalidhan	(*In a hoarse tone*) Fine. Let me pay you first. First let me pay you.

He takes out a wad of notes from the cash-box, counts them and hands them over to Haru Dutta.

	Count it.
Haru Dutta	(*Counts*) Do I have to count? Five, ten, fifty, fifty, five thousand, five thousand and... how much have you given?
Kalidhan	...and five hundred.
Haru Dutta	...and five hundred. This is what you are giving to me now.
Kalidhan	Yes, you keep a note of it.
Haru Dutta	(*Alarmed*) No need. It is enough if you keep a record. I'll leave. (*Gets up*) Its very late now. I don't know if I'll have enough time to go to the

	market and shop. I'm leaving. But what did you decide about that? Do you want to buy some?
Kalidhan	No. It is too expensive.
Haru Dutta	You should keep some, it is excellent stuff. You may never get it again.
Kalidhan	Excellent stuff, but so is the price. And you know what, there is not much profit in it. Rather, you get me some more of this rice.
Haru Dutta	This I will bring for you, but you would have done well to have kept some of that as well. Anyway, I'll let you decide on that, I need to go now.
Kalidhan	Since you insist, bring me some of that.
Haru Dutta	How much?
Kalidhan	How much can you bring?
Haru Dutta	(*Holds up five fingers*) This much.
Kalidhan	(*Appearing surprised*) So much! Fine, bring it.
Haru Dutta	(*Leaving*) Yes, keep some and later decide if you want more. I'm leaving.
Kalidhan	Achha. (*Shouts out*) O Dutta! What did you do with that stuff of mine? That stuff?
Haru Dutta	Which stuff?
Kalidhan	Stuff, do I need to remind you now.

Haru Dutta comes back with a curious look on his face.

Haru Dutta	(*Laughing knowingly*) Tell me. Oho! I remember now. Of course, I'll organize it. I have almost made final arrangements for it. (*Leaving*) It will be done.
Kalidhan	Are you sure?
Haru Dutta	May be within a few... (*Looks back laughing*)

Nabanna ▪ 77

Kalidhan	Are you telling me the truth?
Haru Dutta	See you.
Kalidhan	Achha.

Exit Haru Dutta.

Kalidhan opens the cash-box and fiddles with something in it. Then he pulls out a long key, lies down on his side and unlocks the steel safe beside him. He puts a few wads of notes in it.

Rajib	(*Yawns and snaps his fingers thrice*) Radhe Gobindo! Say Radhe Gobindo!
Kalidhan	Sarkar moshai!

Rajib takes a glance at Kalidhan from under his spectacles and immediately concentrates on his work.

O Sarkar moshai!

Rajib	Speak, I'm listening.
Kalidhan	Did you send the challan in the morning?
Rajib	(*Looks Kalidhan in the eye*) Issued to Bipinbabu? Number twenty-four.
Kalidhan	(*Checks in the notebook*) Right.
Rajib	Yes, I gave it to Rakhahari. Yet you check with him once. If he has actually sent it.
Kalidhan	This is where you create a problem.
Rajib	Why should it be a problem? Here... O what's your name—Rakhahari, Rakhahari. Rakhahari, did you send the challan to Bipinbabu?
Niranjan	(*Leaving aside his work*) What is the challan number?
Kalidhan	Challan number? Are you going to verify the challan number now? No. I'll have to wind up

78 ▪ *Bijon Bhattacharya*

the business.

Enter a bhadralok, suddenly.

	You are?
Bhadralok	I have…
Kalidhan	Yes, yes I remember. Montubabu has sent you. You'll have to wait for a little while; not for long. Please wait just a bit. Please sit.

The bhadralok sits down silently.

(*To Niranjan*) Why are you staring at me like that? What use is it of? The challan has still not been sent. It wasn't sent yesterday. It hasn't been sent today.

Exit Niranjan.

	(*To Rajib*) And you sat quietly having handed the challan to him. You should have checked with him if he had actually sent it. If everyone…
Rajib	I gave it to him right in the morning. If he has not sent it…
Kalidhan	Even if you had given it to him in the morning, you could have checked with him later if he had actually sent it. Then it would have been…
Rajib	I don't have such complexities in my mind.
Kalidhan	It is not a question of complexities. Anyway, there's no point in arguing with you. (*To the bhadralok*) Now tell me what you have to say. O! Sarkar moshai! Did someone come this morning from Anantadham? Do you know?
Rajib	From Anantadham? Yes, yes, someone did

Nabanna ▪ 79

	come, for rice. The amount is…
Kalidhan	(*To the bhadralok, with a smile*) How much rice were you talking about?
Rajib	Wait a moment, let me check the notebook. I had made a note of it.

Looks into the notebook.

Bhadralok	You see, I am an ordinary householder. I have come to you in great need. Of course, I'll pay what you ask for, but I need the rice desperately.
Kalidhan	(*Turns down his hand*) Where will I get rice from? I have had to deny many of my regular customers—people who have been purchasing rice from me for ten–twenty years. You are… No, no I won't be able to help you. You can try elsewhere.
Bhadralok	I will pay the price.
Kalidhan	Then you look for rice elsewhere.
Bhadralok	Please tell me where I should go. I have already been to a few shops and they all say the same thing—there's no rice. Please tell me what I should do. Probably you are not being able to understand my situation. I live in the city. I have to look after many children. There is no rice at home. I hope you can understand.
Kalidhan	I can understand, Moshai. I can understand everything. But is there any way that I can help?
Bhadralok	(*Folding his hands in prayer*) Please do something. You are a Bengali, and I too am a Bengali.
Kalidhan	What price were you mentioning? How much are you willing to pay?

Bhadralok	Price… Whatever you ask for?
Kalidhan	(*Holds up five fingers*) Can you pay this much? If you can, I will try to see if there is some in another shop.
Bhadralok	(*Astonished*) How much! Fifty rupees!
Rajib	(*Looks up*) Don't go on with this. Ask him to leave.
Kalidhan	(*To the bhadralok*) You see!
Rajib	They all want rice. They hunger for rice. They have come for rice. Starved insects!
Kalidhan	(*To the bhadralok*) The very mention of the price shocked you. I had told you at the beginning that you won't be able to afford it.
Bhadralok	But fifty rupees?
Rajib	Arre! We break even at sixty rupees a maun. Did you hear, break even. And you are shocked to hear of fifty.
Kalidhan	(*To the bhadralok, laughing*) You say you want rice, but for payment…
Bhadralok	Are you laughing?
Rajib	Why? Should he cry? Strange!
Bhadralok	Earlier I had paid thirty rupees, now I can pay forty at most. Please let me have at least fifteen seers of rice, I am in great distress.
Rajib	Look here, just listen to what this fellow is saying. The way people behave…
Kalidhan	(*To the bhadralok*) Please excuse me, I won't be able to help you.
Bhadralok	(*With folded hands*) Please give me at least fifteen seers of rice.
Rajib	Look at his audacity. He just won't stop!

	Is he a human?
Bhadralok	(*Angry*) Please shut up. I have been listening to you for long.
Rajib	Look at him make a face! Rakhahari, just throw him out of the shop by his collar. Rakhahari just…
Bhadralok	You are a murderer! I will hand you over to the police, just wait.
Kalidhan	Go, go and call the police. Go!
Bhadralok	(*Frustrated*) When someone comes from Anantadham you can supply as much rice as asked for, but…
Kalidhan	You are shouting unnecessarily. There is no rice. You will not get rice.
Rajib	(*Faking laughter*) Are these people mad, Kalidhan? Says he'll call the police. (*To the bhadralok*) He'll call the police. Arre! Do you have any idea how many judges and magistrates are at babu's beck and call? Idiot. You are trying to threaten him!

(*Cries of 'Maago!' 'Maago!' within. Kalidhan laughs. His belly shakes as he laughs.*)

Bhadralok	(*Angry*) Achha! I am leaving, but I will look for ways to redress this. Once… (*But he cries out helplessly and Kalidhan laughs as his belly shakes.*) But what can I do!

Exit Bhadralok.

Rajib	(*Looking into the cash register*) All the beggars following the famine are swarming to the city,

> they come to their death. Rakhahari, shut the gate, shut the gate…

Loud sound of a collapsible gate being shut.

Curtains

Scene Two

A section of a park. A bench in the corner. About twenty-five beggars sit in a huddle. Pradhan, Kunja, Radhika and Binodini can be seen among the crowd. Pradhan is sewing a torn shirt. Radhika runs her fingers through her hair. Kunja sits with his cheeks resting on his hands, contemplating. Binodini is seen engaged in gossip with another beggar. All belongings are wrapped up in gunny sacks—mud pots, tin cans, etc., lie scattered all over. People of all ages—old, middle-aged, young, children—all are here. Some of them laugh, some cry and some are engaged in a furious row. In the middle of the chaos, a photographer, in western attire, steps in from among the audience and advances towards a beggarwoman with a child.

1st Photographer Bah! Fine model. (*To his colleague*) Come on Mr Mukherjee, let us click a few shots for our daily. You wouldn't find such a model easily, come along.

Another press photographer advances towards the stage from the auditorium.

2nd Photographer Good idea, wait I'm coming. It is an excellent idea that you have come up with. Oh!

Both of them get onto the stage. The 1st Photographer stands at the front-left of the stage and aims his camera at the destitutes.

	How many have you clicked?
1st Photographer	I have clicked two, but I don't think I got the right exposure.
2nd Photographer	Why did you not get it right?
1st Photographer	I am a bit uncertain. The bitch is moving constantly. She did not let me take position.
2nd Photographer	Wait, let me set it right. (*Moves towards the beggars*) And Roy, there is no point in going on clicking 'mob' photographs and wasting film roll. Rather you should choose models and then click. I'll set it. Right, do it like that. (*Spots a woman carrying a little boy*) Hey you, did you get food? I mean, khichdi, did you get khichdi?
Beggarwoman	Where? No.
2nd Photographer	(*Appearing surprised*) Really!

The Beggarwoman makes a pitiful face as she stretches out her hand towards the photographer.

1st Photographer	(*Aiming the lens*) Mukherjee!
2nd Photographer	What?
1st Photographer	Can you get her to smile a bit? Just a bit. Please try.
2nd Photographer	Smile!
1st Photographer	Yes, yes. Then we can use the title 'Bengal Madonna'.
2nd Photographer	What an idea! Circulation will double

	tomorrow. Ofh! Boss will be very pleased with you.
1st Photographer	Isn't it a fantastic idea?
2nd Photographer	But whose idea was it? Now how does one get her to smile?
1st Photographer	Try, please try, just a little bit. Give her some paise if that will work.

Aims his lens.

The 2nd Photographer gets closer to the Beggarwoman.

Beggarwoman	It's not for me, baba; for this little boy. Please have pity.
2nd Photographer	(*With a show of concern*) Do you want money? Here, take!

Gives a coin.

The Beggarwoman's face lights up.

	Roy!
1st Photographer	Okay.
2nd Photographer	What? Was it successful?
1st Photographer	Most likely, let's see. (*Goes up to the Beggarwoman*) Okay, you may go now, go. You've got the money. Now go.

The Beggarwoman moves away.

(*Pitifully*) Really! Mukherjee, just try to get a couple of more models like this one. (*Spots Pradhan*) Yes, that old man. Can you get him to pose? Why don't you try speaking to him. Just try it?

Nabanna ▪ 85

2nd Photographer	Whom do you mean?
1st Photographer	Arre! That old man there. He is sewing something.
2nd Photographer	O! That 'Great Patriarch'!
1st Photographer	Bah! That will make a great title. Truly 'the Great Patriarch'. A fine title. Let's speak to the old man. (*Moves closer to Pradhan*) Hey! Where are you from?
Pradhan	Er-r-r home? Home er-r-r, will you know?
1st Photographer	Yes, of course, we will know the place.
Pradhan	Then I'll tell you. I am from Aminpur.

Laughs.

1st Photographer	Aminpur?
Pradhan	Yes.
1st Photographer	So this place has suited you well for shelter and food.
Pradhan	Suited us! What do we know of convenience…
1st Photographer	Why is that? Achha, can you stand up a bit?
Pradhan	You want me to stand?
1st Photographer	Yes, yes. Just for a bit. We will click a photo.
Pradhan	Photo!
1st Photographer	Yes, photo…like…
Pradhan	Photo of what?
1st Photographer	(*To Mukherjee*) Deal with him.
2nd Photographer	(*To Pradhan*) Your photo. It will be published in the newspaper. We are from the press.

Pradhan	In the newspaper? My photo in the newspaper? But what's the use?
2nd Photographer	What else? People will see it, and learn of the state of the country.
Pradhan	State of the country! So how will they get hold of the newspaper?
2nd Photographer	They will purchase it, of course.
Pradhan	They will buy it?
2nd Photographer	Yes.
Pradhan	You will sell them!
2nd Photographer	Sell…yes, of course. How will people get the paper if it is not sold?
Pradhan	O! That is true! Good, good you sell photos of skeletons and people buy them. Commerce in pictures of skeletons. So, what do I have to do now?
1st Photographer	You just need to stand up. Just a bit.
Pradhan	Stand up! Like this.
2nd Photographer	Yes, stand like that. We will pay you. We'll give money.
Pradhan	Money! You will give me money. Should I take this pot in my hand? This earthen pot? It will look good. It will look very good.
2nd Photographer	The pot…in your hand… (*on being prompted by the 1st Photographer*) Fine, take it, take it.
Pradhan	(*Getting up*) Yes, I'll take it, I'll take it. Let me stand with this pot. Here, now you can click your photograph. Picture of a skeleton. Come on…

2nd Photographer	Roy! Roy! Get ready.
Pradhan	Take the picture of a skeleton.
1st Photographer	(*Clicking photographs. Laughs*) That's it, it did not take long.
Pradhan	Over!
1st Photographer	Yes, dada. We are done. It is just a matter of seconds. Here take this, we had promised to give you some money.
Pradhan	Yes, you had promised to give me money. Give me money.
1st Photographer	(*Gives money*) Here it is. Happy? Achha! 'The Great Patriarch'.

Exit photographers.

Pradhan	Go sell pictures of this skeleton. Go! Go!

He gets back to sewing. Sound of drum rolling within. An announcement can be heard. Soon a Dom[98] enters beating a drum.

Dom	(*Striking the drum thrice*) Bajaarkhola-me khichdi will be served. All beggar-log, go to Bajaarkhola.

He strikes the drum thrice.

A Beggar	(*Curious*) Where baba? Where will they give khichdi?
Dom	Bajaarkhola, Bajaarkhola. (*Strikes the drum thrice*) Bajaarkhola-me khichdi will be served. All beggar-people, go to Bajaarkhola. (*Strikes the drum thrice*)

The announcement creates a buzz among the destitutes. They quickly pick up their meagre belongings and proceed to Bajaarkhola.

Radhika (*Shouts out*) O Bino, Bino re! (*To Kunja*) O go, where's Bino! O Bino…
Kunja Who knows, she may already be waiting there. Nonsense…
Radhika O ma, she should have told us before she went.

Except a few destitutes including Pradhan, others exit quickly.

Pradhan places a torn blanket, a shirt and a whole lot of material on himself and imitates the Dom.

Pradhan Khichdi[99] will be served at Bajaarkhola. All of you go to Bajaarkhola. Dum, dum, dum. All of you go to Bajaarkhola. Dum, dum, dum, dum.

Exit Pradhan.

Enter Tout. He is slim and has drooling eyes. He enters the park, sits on a bench in the corner and lights a cigarette.

Enter Binodini hurriedly.

Bino O ma, where has everyone gone?

The Tout smiles.

What should I do? Babu, do you know anything. I had gone out to beg. Now I find everyone has gone away. Where should I go?
Tout It is very difficult to say where exactly they have gone.
Bino Hai hai hai hai, what will I do now?
Tout Who was with you?

Bino   What did you say, babu?
Tout   I asked you if there were any family members with you?

Binodini doesn't answer.

                   Do you have a husband?
Binodini   I had one. He's abandoned me.
Tout   Abandoned you? Such a pretty face you are, and he's abandoned you. Left you all by yourself? It is grave injustice. There is no dearth of evil men in this city. This is a very serious situation.
Bino   (*Almost in tears*) What should I do, babu?
Tout   You are a woman, what else can I ask you to do?
Bino   Babu, please help me find my people.
Tout   Now how will I find anyone in this big city? So many people have taken shelter here. If only I knew them by their faces. It is impossible to find anyone here. Searching for someone is not easy. See dear, let me tell you what I can do for you. I know a bhadralok in this area. If you want, I can organize a shelter for you in his house. You can do some household chores and they will feed you twice a day. Babu is a very kind man, like Shib[100]... for a few days, while I search for your people. What do you want to do?
Bino   Babu, you are my ma-baap.

The Tout stands up.

Tout   You will have no difficulties there. You can eat and sleep to your heart's content. But the babu is a very wealthy man. He may express a few desires from time to time. Otherwise he is a very nice man. If you can please him… Come on, come along. You are very fortunate, what else can I say. Come along, come along…

Exit.

Curtains

Scene Three

On the right—a city road. The house of a rich man. Well-dressed men and women enter and leave through the main entrance. Inside, a row of fine wooden chairs are lit up by electric lamps. Shehnai being played inside the house—Raag Ashavari. A group of young women go out of the gate laughing cheerfully. The master of the household stands in front of the gate along with others. He is greeting the guests, 'Please come in. Have a seat.' A pretty girl stands beside him with a load of bael flower garlands. On the left corner is a dustbin, barely visible. Radhika and Kunja search for food among the rubbish. It is dark and nothing is clearly visible. The growling of a dog can be heard from around the dustbin. Pradhan can be seen. He stands at a little distance from the gate of the said building appealing for a bit of rice. A little later, Radhika too can be seen with greater clarity. She too pleads fervently for rice. Suddenly, a dog starts barking ferociously near the dustbin. Almost immediately Kunja responds in screaming in bestial anger. In a few moments, Kunja advances towards the light holding up his wounded hand—bitten by the dog and dripping with blood. (It is advisable that a spotlight be used to highlight this episode.)

Master Householder (*Greets a guest with a garland*) Please, please come in. (*With a smile*) Hehe! Come in.

The 1st Bhadralok responds with a namaskar and enters the house. Behind him the 2nd and 3rd Bhadraloks enter chatting among themselves.

2nd Bhadralok Do you know what the real issue is? It's money, money. Money can get you everything. None of our Bengali businessmen have any capital. Go to Bombay or Ahmedabad, you'll see...

Smiles as he meets the Master Householder.

Arre! Are we late?

Master Householder (*Smiles*) Arre, come, come, come in. And where is Mukherjee? Didn't you get Nirmalbabu with you?

2nd Bhadralok (*Raising his hand*) Yes, yes, everyone is here. (*Looks behind in surprise*) Arre, where are you, Mukherjee, why are you lagging behind?

3rd Bhadralok So Baro babu, you seem to be doing very well. Oo! He he he he.

Cries of distress within.[101]

Enter Nirmalbabu.

Nirmalbabu (*Comes forward*) Here I am, Dada.
2nd Bhadralok Arre, Nirmalbabu, come in, come, come...
3rd Bhadralok It is impossible to move around in this blackout, and...
Master Householder Don't even mention it. There is the

	blackout on the one hand and this horrible weather on the other. Maybe it is just my fate. Now if we can get through…
2nd Bhadralok	That is right! And how many guests do you have?
Master Householder	That would be around a thousand. I tried a lot to leave people out, but could not reduce it any further.
3rd Bhadralok	A complete thousand. Really! Thousand instead of fifty. You may be prosecuted under the Defence of India Act![102]
Master Householder	Hah! There are such laws and there are the loopholes as well! (*Laughs*) And how would I reduce it further? The list of friends and relations itself extends beyond five hundred. Besides…

Cries of distress within.

2nd Bhadralok	That is true. It is no big deal. What else can one do? Last April, I had organized the first rice ceremony for my grandson. It is not a major function like a wedding. Yet I had invited at least eight hundred people despite all my efforts to reduce the guest list. And you are inviting people for a wedding ceremony.
Nirmalbabu	So this is a royal affair you have organized, Roymoshai. Oha! Feeding a thousand guests in such times, it's not a small matter.
2nd Bhadralok	Imagine!

Nabanna ▪ 93

Nirmalbabu	Did you manage to find everything? Was there any trouble?
Master Householder	Trouble? Black market. As long as there is a black market...
2nd Bhadralok	What else can be done? To tell you the truth, it is only because of the black market that we are surviving, or else what would have people done? There is no other way but to approach the black market. Simple things, like sugar... At home, my wife says she needs at least one and half maunds of sugar every month, or else—you can understand—all will come to a standstill. Now, where will you find sugar? Go to the open market. You won't find any sugar. Nothing at all. All shopkeepers keep saying the same thing—there is no stock. Where will you get sugar from? What else can you do? Let the black market thrive. Let the hoarder thrive. You may have to pay four times the price, but you will get your stuff. What else will you do? Money won't follow you after your death.
Nirmalbabu	People who have money may hold such views! The trouble is that most people do not have that kind of money.

Cries of distress within.

2nd Bhadralok	Nirmalbabu, it is not possible to engage in such deep thinking, I am unable to think

	so much. There are lakhs and lakhs of cases of injustice in society every day. If we are to protest against each and every instance of injustice, we have to abandon our jobs, trade and commerce.
Nirmalbabu	Give it up if you have to—but should we be silent in the face of injustice?
2nd Bhadralok	Give up business! What are you saying? (*Laughs*) You've cracked a good joke, Nirmalbabu.

The Master Householder, the 3rd Bhadralok and others share a hearty laugh.

Master Householder Come, let's go in.

Exit.

Immediately the spotlight is focussed above the dustbin. The dog barks ferociously. A scream—probably the dog has bitten someone. Kunja comes forward with his bloodied hand.

Pradhan	(*From the darkness*) Babu, o Babu, please give some rice, some rice...
Radhika	(*In dread*) O ma! It's bitten you!

Radhika runs towards Kunja from the dustbin.

Radhika	(*To the dog*) It is an evil dog. It's bitten him! Go away, you awful dog. Hit it with a broom, hit it. I'll make you eat ash. Go, thu thu thu...

She spits out in anger and frustration. Growling of the dog heard within.

Nabanna ▪ 95

Kunja   O ma! It has bitten off quite a bit. O ma! What will happen to me! Ishh...sh...sh.

She tears off a bit of the cloth she is wearing and ties it as a bandage over Kunja's wound.

Pradhan   (*Wears a loin cloth as he raises his arms and shouts at the house*) How much longer do I have to shout out for a little bit of rice! Have all of you become deaf? Can't you hear? Don't you have a heart? O Baba, o Babu—you waste so much of food, and throw away so much. But you are unable to give a fistful of rice to this old starving man. Don't you have any mercy! O Baba, o Babu!

Exit.

Radhika   (*Tying the bandage over Kunja's wounded arm*) It must be paining! Do you want some water to drink? Should I get you some water? Water?

Kunja   No.

Kunja looks on at Radhika with tears in his eyes. Radhika, having finished tying the bandage, looks at Kunja. Her eyes fill up with tears as she remembers something. Radhika brushes away the hair from Kunja's forehead with great tenderness. She starts to cry. Kunja stares at her as he lifts his left hand and places it over Radhika's head.

Curtains

Scene Four

Haru Dutta's house. It is afternoon. Haru Dutta squats on a stool in the verandah in front of his house, smoking the hookah. Three young rustic women sit at one corner of the verandah, with their heads covered by their sarees. Two of them sit with their backs towards the audience. The third—Khuki's Mother—a child widow, sits facing Haru Dutta and speaks on without any modesty. Another elderly rustic man (Chander) sits in the courtyard.

Haru Dutta	(*Drawing his hookah*) What I have done for the village is known to everyone and (*looks up*) to God. What more can I say? I have never had the habit of self-praise.
Khuki's Mother	You don't need to talk about it. We know it all. (*To the elderly man*) When Khuki had fallen ill, when was that…in the month of Karthik. The time when I sold off ten bamboo stems through you Haro's father.
Chander	(*With a worried look*) Eight, not ten.
Khuki's Mother	Ten. No, I remember it clearly. I sold ten bamboo stems to you. The price came to three rupees and two annas. You gave me three rupees. You did not have change, so you did not give me the two annas. Later the two annas were adjusted against paddy. Do you remember?
Chander	(*Shakes his head*) Yes, yes. It was my mistake. You are right, you are right.
Haru Dutta	(*Raises his head*) Khuki's Mother, you

Nabanna ▪ 97

	should have been a pleader at the Judge's Court.
Khuki's Mother	(*Laughs*) Baba, didn't you say that women of the modern day are learned and are competing with men in all spheres of work. If I had received that kind of education, with your blessings, I would have made all the judges and the advocates swoon.
Haru Dutta	(*Forced laughter*) You would have, Khuki's Mother, you are capable of doing so. (*Lifts his hand affectionately as if he is about to slap Khuki's Mother from a distance*) You are...you are very naughty!
Khuki's Mother	Let that be. As I was saying, when Khuki was ill for about fifteen days I was in a very sorry state. I did not know what to do. I ran to Doctor Ramnath. I requested him repeatedly, and fell at his feet to examine the child one last time. But no. He wanted to be paid first. He might well have been a dacoit. I pleaded with him, I don't have money today, I will pay you in a few days. He did not budge. I wondered what to do. Whom to go to? Then I thought of Baba, and I ran to him. I am telling you the truth, even if you think I am exaggerating. But here I touch Baba's feet as I recount this—I am not making up even a bit. God is a witness to everything. (*Closing her eyes*) How can I express it, Baba understood everything

just by taking one look at me. I did not have to tell him everything. He came to my home, gave some medicines, and in three days my daughter returned from death's door. In fact, the day Khuki was to return to normal diet, Baba brought rice for her. He said, 'Khuki's Mother, you may not have good rice at home, you feed this to Khuki.' And it wasn't a small amount—at least two seers. Whenever I have approached Baba for some help, he has never refused. And it is not just my story, whoever has come to him, whoever! So what you have done for us, we know very well. You need not repeat.

Haru Dutta (*Lifts his head from the hookah*) This is nothing. Nothing. I will help you in your distress, you will support me in my days of trouble. How else can we survive, isn't it Chander?

Chander What you have said is right. What can be wrong in it?

Haru Dutta Why do you think I am arranging for your journey? Why do I need to do this for all of you? Just because I won't be able to tolerate the sight of everyone starving to death. Or else, what is in it for me? Why should I spend my money to do this for you? Taking all the trouble of organizing people to help you. There's no gain for me in this charity. Of course, you can

	turn around and say that I need not have made this effort…
Chander	No, no one can say that!
Haru Dutta	I said that only for the sake of argument. Everyone is not like me, isn't it? There are a lot of evil people in this world. They can say whatever they want. Can you prevent them, Chander? It is said that all should beware of the tiger that shakes its tail slowly, for it is a man-eater. Such people may say, 'You need not engage in charity. Who's asked you to make the effort?' Will you be able to answer them? If everyone was mean like them, the human society would have been destroyed a long time ago.
Chander	(*Looks at Haru Dutta in surprise*) Everything would have been destroyed!
Khuki's Mother	Hoon hoon. (*Smiles and nods her head*)
Haru Dutta	But everyone is not evil. There are good people too. (*Emphatically*) They are the ones managing this world. Chander, there is a lot more to know about in this world, a great deal more. Anyway, now quickly put your thumb impression here.
Chander	Do I need to put my thumb impression?
Haru Dutta	Ore baba re, of course you have to. Always remember, Chander, that oral agreements have no value. They last as long as the speech itself. Whatever you do, you should do it on paper. The

agreement gets frozen forever. Come on, do it quickly. I have to go. Come on, where are you?

Chander walks up to Haru Dutta and puts his thumb impression on a piece of paper.

Press it hard, oho! It is smudged. That will do. It won't matter. (*Examines the thumb impression*) See, it did not take much effort.

Chander   (*Emotional*) Baba, please look after my daughter...she shouldn't...

Chander chokes.

Haru Dutta   Do not worry. I have taken the responsibility...

Chander   Do you know, Baba, the girl lost her mother at the age of three. Since then I have raised her almost single-handedly. (*Wipes his tears*) I no longer have anything to be proud of. (*Breaks down crying*)

Haru Dutta   (*Shows being hurt*) Why are you so concerned about your daughter? Is she just your daughter, not mine?

Khuki's Mother   (*To Chander*) Why are you crying? Your daughter will be fine.

Haru Dutta   Ai, where are you?

Someone answers within, 'Coming, Babu'.

To hell with 'Coming Babu'. Has the boat been docked?

Nabanna ▪ 101

Servant	(*Enthusiastically*) Should I load the boat?
Haru Dutta	'Should I load'? What have you been doing all this while? You have been gone long!
Servant	Babu, I had gone to fetch the boat to the ghat.
Haru Dutta	O! So should I be eternally indebted to you? You son of a bitch! How long does it take to fetch the boat. How many days does it take to walk to the ghat? And how dare you answer back? Look down, look down, you dirty rodent! If we're unable to reach by daylight you will face the music.
Servant	It is low tide, we will move quicker.
Haru Dutta	If we have to move, why are you still standing here like an ethereal beauty? Move!

Servant moves towards exit.

	And listen…ask them to put three oars in place.
Servant	It is low tide, we would be able to make it with two oars.
Haru Dutta	No, you don't have to make it. Do as I say. Tell them to fix three oars.

Exit Servant.

Holds the hookah as he speaks to the women.

So go ahead all of you. Move ahead. Khuki's Mother, take all of them with you.

The women exit.

> Chander, here's your money. (*Takes out a purse from the folds of his cloth and counts notes*) Take it.

Chander hesitates and ponders before taking the money.

> This much is for now. Let me return, I will give you some more. (*Draws some smoke from the hookah.*)

Chander   I have sold my daughter! I have sold Mati. (*Crying*) My dearest Mati, Matangini…

Exit Chander.

Haru Dutta sits on a two-foot-high stool, smoking his hookah.

Curtains

Scene Five

A room in an ashram. Binodini stands at the window holding onto the iron bars of the window grill. Niranjan sits on the floor in the middle of the room. He stares at the floor with fury in his eyes. He appears vengeful.

Binodini wears a soiled saree. Niranjan, barefoot, wears a short half shirt and a soiled dhoti. They seem to be misfits in their current surroundings.

Binodini   (*Turning around suddenly, in rage*) And that's not all. I can't even explain the torture.

Nabanna ▪ 103

Niranjan	(*Rubs his fist*) I shall have my revenge. (*Lets out a sigh in frustration*) Achha!
Binodini	(*Hoarse voice*) Makhan was on his deathbed, Didi was sick, your brother was knocking about from place to place like a madman.
Niranjan	(*As if returning to his senses*) Dada!
Binodini	He went all over, scouting fervently for some medicine, for some food and your Jetha—the less said about his condition the better. Every waking hour he rants about Shripati and Bhupati. Even when it is pitch dark, snakes creeping about, the deathly wind blowing in from the burning ghats, when no one dares venture out—the old man goes out into the woods. He says, 'Let me go search for my Shripati and my Bhupati.' To witness his condition is painful. And in this state, that man Dutta inflicted tremendous torture on them. I shall never forget it in my life.
Niranjan	Wasn't there anyone in the village who would speak up?
Binodini	There were, but who dares utter a word against Dutta? Whoever speaks will be murdered.
Niranjan	(*In rage*) Murderer! I will seek out that murderer… (*Starts pacing up and down*)

Enter Rajib.

Rajib	(*Speaking to Niranjan*) Ah! Don't you flex your muscles… (*Surprised as he spots Binodini*) Who is this? Rakhahari! (*To Binodini*) Why are you here? What are you doing here? Don't you know that

Babu will be extremely angry if he finds you here. Go in. I am telling you to go inside. Go!

Binodini lowers her head and exits.

Rakhahari! Why did she have to come scooting into this room and whisper to this man… you there, why don't you speak up?

Niranjan Who came scooting into the room?

Rajib You know very well who I'm talking about? Stupid man! What were you telling her? You thought you could fool this old man, haan? He's found a nice place for courtship…

Niranjan Don't shout like a vulture. We're speaking of other things.

Rajib (*Shrugs his shoulders*) What did you say? Vulture, I shout like a vulture! Wait, I will straighten you up and your crooked words. (*Turns around*) A dirty fox is stealing the lions' share. Just wait and watch what Babu does to you today. Just look at the audacity of the bloody knave!

Enter Kalidhan, in great haste.

Kalidhan Sarkar moshai, wait! Don't go! (*To Niranjan*) Wait! (*To Rajib*) I have heard everything from Gyanoda. Sarkar moshai, tell me what has happened. Tell me, there is no need of hiding anything from me.

Rajib (*Scratches his head*) What should I say? Aye Rakhahari, why are you mum? Speak up!

Kalidhan (*To Niranjan*) Aren't you aware that this is an ashram?

Nabanna ▪ 105

Rajib I have always told you Kalidhan that you should not give any leeway to these worthless people. But you won't listen to me. And are these scums human beings at all?

Niranjan glares at Rajib.

Kalidhan (*To Niranjan*) Get out! Get out I say! Get out of here this very moment! I don't need a worker like you around. (*Threatens*) You just get lost!

Exit Niranjan.

Enter Binodini, in great haste.

Binodini I want to go. Let me go. Leave me, let me go.
Rajib (*Stops her*) What are you doing? You are a woman. You should be indoors. What do you want to go out for? Go inside, strange!
Binodini Leave me, let me go. I want to go. Let me go!
Kalidhan Gyanoda!

Enter Gyanoda.

(*Points towards Binodini*) Take her inside.
Gyanoda (*Drags Binodini by her hand*) Come, don't behave like that, come in now!

Exit Binodini with Gyanoda.

Rajib proceeds to exit.

Kalidhan Sarkar moshai! Settle his dues immediately. We can't keep him here. We can't keep traitors here.
Rajib That's exactly what I say. I tell you again, don't

106 ▪ *Bijon Bhattacharya*

	encourage such vermins. These are not even human beings.
Kalidhan	Achha, you don't need to advise me on that. Go in and do as I say.
Rajib	I am going, what is it to me? I am going.

Exit.

Kalidhan	Yes, you go now. What trouble! Let me sit down for a while… And whom can one rely on? All of them are nincompoops.

Lies down on a cushioned easy chair.

Is anyone there?

Enter Servant.

Servant	(*Salutes*) Babu.
Kalidhan	What do all of you do sitting there all the time? Why don't you respond when you are called?
Servant	Ji, I came immediately.
Kalidhan	Immediately?
Servant	Ji…
Kalidhan	Shut up! Who was at the gate in the afternoon?
Servant	I was at the gate in the afternoon.
Kalidhan	When did Rakhahari come here?
Servant	Ji, he came within daylight.
Kalidhan	Within daylight!
Servant	Ji.
Kalidhan	Hoon, but he should never be allowed to enter the premises again.
Servant	Not allow him to enter!
Kalidhan	What else did I tell you? Don't allow him.
Servant	Ji, as you order.

Nabanna ▪ 107

Kalidhan	Don't allow anyone in without my orders.
Servant	Ji.
Kalidhan	And as soon as Ramratanbabu arrives, let me know.

Clanking of horses within. The Servant looks in that direction.

	What are you looking there for?
Servant	Ji, someone seems to have arrived in a carriage.
Kalidhan	In a carriage?
Servant	(*Looking into the wings*) Ji, I'm not able to recognize anyone. But a few days back a Babu in a suit had paid a visit. This person looks quite like him. And there are two. (*Looks carefully*) Yes, two. There are two ladies with him.
Kalidhan	Ladies too. (*Gets up*) Ladies in a carriage? Who can it be? Come, let's have a look.

Enter Niranjan and Binodini.

Exit Kalidhan and Servant.

Binodini	(*In a low, fearful voice*) Who are they?
Niranjan	(*Puts his finger on his lips*) Quiet! It is that Haru Dutta.
Binodini	Haru Dutta!
Niranjan	Shhhh... This Babu is his Mahajan, which is why he often visits this place. But the girls...

Looks on in surprise.

Binodini	Who are they?
Niranjan	I am unable to figure it out. But they seem to be familiar. Where have I seen them? I can't

	remember. But since it is Dutta who's got them here, they must be from our village. Scoundrels. That's right. I've got it, I got to trap all of them.
Binodini	(*Confused*) What are you going to do?
Niranjan	Nothing. You keep quiet. Now listen to me. Go right in and remain there quietly. No need to speak to anyone about anything. Complete silence. I am leaving.
Binodini	Okay…but where are you going?
Niranjan	I'll tell you later, but remember what I told you. Now go, quick.

Exit Niranjan.

Enter Gyanoda.

Gyanoda	O ma, what will I do! Why are you standing here, alone, like this? Go in, go in. The bhadraloks will all be here. Go in.

Exit Binodini.

	(*Looks out with eyes wide open*) Who has come now, who? (*Unable to ascertain*) Anyway, what does it all matter to me… I need not bother.

Kalidhan and Haru Dutta enter hand in hand.

Exit Gyanoda.

Kalidhan	(*Laughs*) I've been wondering, it seemed Dutta was gone forever. And there were no letters from you. Who's there? Bring the hookah.
Haru Dutta	(*Smiles*) Say no more of that. I didn't manage to find time all day in procrastination. On the one

Nabanna ▪ 109

	hand is the mahajan's demands for repayment, on the other, contractor keeps demanding more, and then there is... (*Laughs*) I've been too busy.
Kalidhan	You are a superman, Haru Dutta. How do you manage so many things at once. Not a matter of joke.
Haru Dutta	You've got to manage, got to manage. One has to work to survive.
Kalidhan	(*Laughing*) Ooo...what a thing you've said. Where do we stand then!
Haru Dutta	(*Pokes Kalidhan in the thigh*) Come on... don't talk like that.
Kalidhan	Anyway, I say now you should get a house in the city. I can arrange one at a cheap price. I know people.

In a show of endearment, Kalidhan strokes Haru Dutta's chin.

Haru Dutta	(*Surprised*) Residing in the city. No, not for me. We are, what you call, born rustic. We won't be able to handle life in the city.

A servant brings in hookahs for them.

Kalidhan	(*Shoves Haru Dutta*) What is a born rustic! (*Mock laughter*) But our rustic ways are in no way any lesser than the ways of the city. (*More laughter*) Uri-i baba, you make such amazing statements.

But soon the smile on their faces disappear, as a Police Inspector and a couple of constables enter, along with Niranjan and a few gentlemen.

Inspector	Are you Kalidhan Dhara?
Kalidhan	(*Looking up at the Inspector*) Yes, I am but…

Looks towards Haru Dutta.

Inspector	Are you surprised?

Kalidhan and Haru Dutta stand up in a state of shock. Haru Dutta's eyes light up in fear.

Kalidhan	What brings you here?
Inspector	Are you unable to figure that out? (To Haru Dutta) What's your name?
Haru Dutta	Shit! (*Turning towards the Inspector, confused*) You want to know my name?
Inspector	Yes, yes, what is your name?
Haru Dutta	My name is Haran Chandra Dutta.
1st Bhadralok	Haran Chandra Dutta! Lord Krishna had a hundred names.
Inspector	Haran Chandra Dutta, also known as Haru Dutta. Right?
Haru Dutta	(*Astonished*) Ji, yes.
Inspector	Hoon! (*To Kalidhan and Haru Dutta*) Where have you kept the girls?
Kalidhan	(*Feigning surprise*) Girls? What are you saying, sir? This is a sebashram.
Inspector	Yes, can't there be girls in a sebashram? Particularly since you are an enterprising lot. Quick. Let us know where you've kept them, or else you'll be in a lot of trouble.
1st Bhadralok	I see, along with rice and grains, he has dug his hands into other kinds of trade. He is a murderer!

Inspector	Speak up! (*To Rakhahari*) You go in. Take the constables to the girls. Get them here.
Niranjan	Please come with me.

Exit Niranjan and the Constables.

Bhadralok	Ooh! A great arrangement for quick profiting. Along with rice he has… yes, this is the same man who had refused to sell me rice the other day. However, he must have hoarded tonnes of rice in his godown. If you ask him for some, he will turn his hand over and claim there's none. Cheat!

The Inspector notes everything.

Kalidhan	Go on, say what you want. Since our words have no value, you can say whatever you want.
Bhadralok	'No value!' Do you deserve any 'value'? Murderers, all! (*To the Inspector*) Have you seen, how they try to appear as if they are saints, and we are the ones who are inflicting torture on them? Oh! You are seasoned fraudsters.
Inspector	(*To the Bhadralok*) Aah!

Enter Niranjan, Chander's daughters, Binodini, Gyanoda, Rajib, the Constables and a Servant.

	The entire lot!
Niranjan	No (*Pointing out Chander's two daughters*), the two of them are from our village. Dutta has kidnapped them.
Haru Dutta	I have not kidnapped them.
Inspector	You shut up! (*To Niranjan*) Go on, finish what

112 ▪ *Bijon Bhattacharya*

	you have to say.
Niranjan	(*Pointing out Binodini*) And she is my wife. She came to the city to escape starvation. This Babu's people spotted her and got her here. I worked as a manager in his shop. I met her, all of a sudden one day, and asked her what she was doing here…
Inspector	Anyway, we'll listen to that narrative sometime later. As of now let us note that you claim that she is your wife, right?
Niranjan	Ji, I swear she is. (*To Binodini*) Why don't you tell them?

Binodini stands in attention.

Inspector	(*Smile*) Let that be. And you claim that you worked as a manager for the Babu?
Niranjan	Ji, in his rice godown.
Inspector	Godown—you mean his shop?
Niranjan	Yes, actually my work was in his godown.
Inspector	Godown. So how much rice does he have there right now?

There is a flutter in Kalidhan's face.

Niranjan	It is many a maund.
Inspector	Is there an estimate of how much you mean by 'many maunds'?
Niranjan	Should be about one-and-a-quarter lakh maunds.
Inspector	One-and-a-quarter lakh!
Niranjan	(*Irked*) This is an estimate. It can be lesser or more.

Inspector	That's all right! (*To Niranjan, pointing at Rajib*) Who is he?
Niranjan	He is Babu's right hand man, Sarkar moshai.
Bhadralok	(*Sarcastically*) He also claims that Babu purchased all judges and magistrates.
Inpector	Is that so?
Rajib	What? I never said any such thing.
Inspector	You shut up! (*To the constables*) Put handcuffs on the three of them.

The constables put handcuffs on Kalidhan, Haru Dutta and Rajib. Haru Dutta and Kalidhan keep looking at each other expressing through gestures that it was only a matter of time before they would walk free again.

Curtains

Act Three

Scene One

As announced by a poster on a pillar, this is a 'Free Kitchen'. A large number of destitute and hungry people sit upstage. They are all talking among themselves, creating a din. Kunja and Radhika can be seen towards the front of the crowd. Suddenly there is a cry of a woman within. Everyone on stage is startled out of fear. Some of them have their eyes wide open and others, their mouths open. An old and sick beggar sits and coughs convulsively and at times lifts his eyes to watch all that's going around him.

1st Beggarwoman   (*As the cries within die down*) Have you seen what they have done? (*To those around her*) If you've got to take her away, take all of them away at once. But no, they will take one person and let the rest be. What a sickening thing to do. (*Shouts out*) They took the girl, but left her mother behind on the streets. Do they have no heart at all!

1st Beggar	(*Anxious*) But why is she shouting like that?
1st Beggarwoman	O ma, won't she shout if they are taking her daughter away? What is he saying… they are taking people away one by one and injecting them, I know that.
An Old Beggar	(*Coughing*) They will take everyone away. No one will be spared. Run where you can, run away everyone. If you thought they would spare you because you are in a shelter, hehehe! (*Laughs*) Don't be mistaken. They will take everyone. Run away now, while there is still time. Run away while you can.
Kunja	Where are they taking them all packed in a lorry?[103]
2nd Beggar	I don't know! Some people say they are being taken to the war. Others are saying that they are sending everyone from farming families back to their villages.
1st Beggarwoman	They are killing many of them with injections.
Kunja	No, that can't be true.
2nd Beggar	You never know, it may be true.
Kunja	Are you mad? The injections that can kill people. It may be poison, but it has a cost. What is the price of our lives—yours and mine? Nothing at all. We will die just like that.
2nd Beggar	So where are they taking them in lorries?
3rd Beggar	I heard many stories. Some say that there

	has been a bumper crop of rice this time and there aren't enough people to harvest. So all farming families are being sent back to the villages.
Kunja	It is better to go on one's own, walking all the way. Why take all the trouble?
2nd Beggar	Yes, who knows where each one will be taken off in the lorry.
Kunja	(*Raises his hand*) This is the opportunity. Let us all go up to the north end. There's no trouble there.
2nd Beggar	Which way did you say?
Kunja	(*Pointing with his hand*) There, to the North.
2nd Beggar	North for you. South for us. Have you heard of Panchmohallah?
Kunja	Panchmohallah?
2nd Beggar	Yes, it is far from here.
The Old Beggar	That is what I keep thinking. I can't move a bit. How will I travel such a great distance? What will happen to me? (*Coughs*) No, I will have to leave my bones right here. (*Screams out in anguish*) All of you go! Go away leaving me behind! Forget me! Forget me!

Bell rings within.

2nd Beggar	They've rung the bell for food, they've rung the bell for food.
1st Beggarwoman	Finally, the bell has rung. Offh! They took almost till eternity to ring the bell today.

Kunja, Radhika, the Old Beggar and others exit with their vessels.

The Old Beggar	(*In anguish*) I won't make it. All of you go on. (*In tune*) Go back to the village.
Kunja	(*To Radhika*) When I try to think of going back to the village, my heart goes… here, just place your hand here, and check my heart, check…
Radhika	(*Worried*) Really!
Kunja	(*Grins lamentably*) Heh! It brings so much joy to me. Come my dear, let us go back to the village. I don't want to be in this dead land anymore. Let's go back.
Radhika	Let's go, I am all for it. It would be a pleasure to return to the village. (*Cries*) But the land there is dead as well… It's just my fate, if Makhan had been alive. (*Crying*)
Kunja	It will all be better, my dear. Don't lose heart. Come, my dear, let us return to the village. We shall not live in this dead city any more.
The Old Beggar	(*In anguish*) Don't cling on to the false promises of the city. Go back, go back, all of you.
Kunja	My dear!
Radhika	What?
Kunja	Get up, let us go!
Radhika	Let us go.

Radhika holds Kunja's hand and stands up.

The Old Beggar   (*In anguish*) The long road goes winding. Go walk ahead. Go back all of you. Go!

Radhika holds Kunja's hand and walks.

Curtains

Scene Two

A charity clinic. Cots are lined up along two walls of a longish room. All cots are occupied. At the centre of the room, a nurse sits at the desk. She rests her elbows on the desk as she holds her head. Medicines, medical equipment and notebooks fill up the desk. Two of the patients make a strange sound in pain. The nurse keeps turning her head towards the patients repeatedly.

Right outside the dormitory is a verandah. A table, two chairs and a bench are placed in the middle of the verandah. A coat hangs from a wooden rack on the wall. A young doctor examines 'Outdoor' patients. Destitute patients crowd the steps to the verandah. A chemist sits at his desk, preparing medicines. Middle-class bhadralok patients are seated on the bench in front of the doctor. They hold bottles of medicine in their hands. There is a ten-year-old boy along with one of the bhadraloks. He wears bandage on his head and face.

A Jemadar—smartly attired with cuffs at his ankles, turban on his head, and a coat on his back—manages the crowd.

A patient, lying towards the back of the dormitory cries out in pain. The nurse gets up and attends to him with medicine. She returns to the table to write something down. Meanwhile some of the other patients cry out louder.

Nurse (*Scolds the patients*) What is the matter!

Having been scolded, the patient at first cot groans before he falls silent. The nurse examines the pulse of the patients, one at a time. Peace returns to the dormitory for a while. After some time, the patient on the second cot groans before she falls silent. The nurse glances at her and carries on with her examination. This is the scene inside the dormitory. In the verandah outside, the doctor—attired in western clothes—examines patients with his stethoscope, places his hands on their back as he instructs them to 'take a deep breath', and writes prescriptions one by one. The patients take the prescriptions and queue up for the medicines. The chemist—attired in a shirt and a dhoti—seems to be working busily at his desk. He pours out medicines into the patients' bottles from large red, blue and white bottles.

Chemist	(*To a patient while pouring out medicine for another patient*) Yours!
Doctor	(*Examining a destitute patient*) Does it pain in the chest when you cough?
Patient No. 8	Yes, Babu, it pains a lot.
Doctor	It pains. What kind of a pain?
Patient No. 8	What kind of a pain? Pain! (*Unable to express himself, casts an empty gaze on the doctor*)
Doctor	Tongue, show me your tongue.

The patient shows his tongue.

> Show it to me, hang it out.
> Unh! (*Notes in the prescription*) Do you get sleep at night?

The patient shakes his head.

	You do not.
Patient No. 8	Ji, no.
Doctor	(*Tears off the prescription from the letter pad and hands it over to the patient*) Okay, continue with the same medicine for another week.
Patient No. 8	Ji, Doctor Babu, you had said that you will change the medicine today.
Doctor	Did I say so? Anyway, let it continue for a week.
Patient No. 8	But the fever has not gone away.
Doctor	It will go, keep taking the medicine. It does not take much time to get infected, but takes a lot of time to get cured. Impatience will not help. (*To another patient*) What about you? (*To Patient No. 8*) Okay, you may go now.
Patient No. 8	The fever won't go, Doctor Babu. Please give me a stronger medicine, Doctor Babu, I beg you.
Doctor	Arre baba! Will I invent a stronger medicine? What I've prescribed is strong enough.
Patient No. 8	I have been taking this medicine for a month, but the fever has not waned. And my feet are swollen still.
Doctor	That medicine will take care of everything.
Patient No. 8	Everything?
Doctor	Yes, everything. Go now, I have a lot more patients to see.
Patient No. 8	I will go then, I will go.

Nabanna ▪ 121

Joins the queue.

Bhadralok Patient	(*He is sitting in front of the doctor's table*) Is it all malaria?
Doctor	Mostly, but not only malaria. This man has oedema. He is suffering for almost a month, but there is no medicine in the store. What can I prescribe?
Bhadralok Patient	So, why don't you let the higher ups know of the situation?
Doctor	I've grown tired of writing. I have told them that if they aren't able to supply medicines they should shut down this 'sham show' in the name of a hospital. But there has been no reply. Can you tell me what more we can do? To attend to the crisis we may work for ten hours instead of two, we may write two hundred prescriptions instead of ten, but in the absence of medicines what use would that be?
Bhadralok Patient	That is true.
Doctor	Even sympathy, when there, goes wasted. This is our tragedy. But let that be. (*To another patient*) What do you have? Show me.

He continues to work at his desk. Suddenly, he raises his head and smiles at the nurse.

	What were you hoping, Reba? That the man would survive?
Nurse	Hope? No, there is no hope.

The doctor concentrates on his work.

Enter Pradhan.

Suddenly the nurse notices an old dishevelled man standing at the door. He looks like a madman. He carries dirty papers under one of his arms and holds a pot in another; he also holds an old, torn cloth and keeps a torn blanket on his shoulders.

	What's the matter with you, now?
Doctor	(*Raises his head*) Who?
Nurse	What do you want?
Pradhan	I want some medicine.
Nurse	Medicine?

Pradhan nods his head.

	Medicine for what?
Doctor	What does he say? Who is it?
Nurse	Just see!
Doctor	(*Gets up*) What happened? What are you trying to say?
Pradhan	(*Comes up*) Give me some medicine, Baba. (*Indicates his feet*) Pains a lot.
Doctor	Pains a lot! Where? Let me take a look. (*Points towards the rubbish on Pradhan's shoulders*) What are these?
Pradhan	It's there.
Doctor	It's just there?
Pradhan	(*Laughs nervously*) Yes, just there.
Doctor	Why don't you throw them away? What use are they?
Pradhan	What will be left if I throw these away? I can't throw them. They are all…

Nabanna ▪ 123

Doctor	Precious possessions. Can't be thrown away?
Pradhan	No. (*Laughs*)
Doctor	(*To the nurse*) Did you understand the nature of his illness?
Nurse	(*Smiles*) A bit.
Doctor	Such illnesses occurred to many, and it is bound to happen.
Pradhan	(*Unable to understand*) It is bound to happen. Why? (*Suddenly feels pain*) Uh! Uh uh! It is paining.
Doctor	Where? Where does it pain?
Pradhan	(*Lifts his foot*) Here. (*Points*) It pains here.
Doctor	(*Examines the foot*) Where is the pain? Does it hurt if I press it?
Pradhan	No.
Doctor	Then where does it pain?
Pradhan	(*Slight laugh*) It was there, right there.
Doctor	It was there?
Pradhan	It was there. Now it's gone. It's run away.

The nurse controls her laughter.

Doctor	It ran away?

Pradhan raises his hands in a victorious posture.

	Where did it go?
Pradhan	(*Moves his limb with vigour*) That pain ran away. Whoosh! It went over the river, the streams, the canal and the forests, that pain ran as fast as the wind behind a car.

Suddenly, he feels pain in another part of his body, holds it and crouches. The doctor looks at the nurse and Pradhan grimaces in pain.

Doctor	(*Slight laugh*) Is it paining again?
Pradhan	(*Serious*) Yes, it is paining again. It is a terrible pain, it hurts. This pain is here now and gone the next moment. This pain comes to my body like the north-westerly storm and breaks in as if destroying all doors and windows…
Doctor	(*Snubs him*) Stop!
Pradhan	(*Politely*) Are you telling me to shut up?
Doctor	Yes, stop. All that talk of pain is nonsense, it is false.
Pradhan	(*Aggrieved*) Nonsense!

A cry of pain from the dormitory. The nurse rushes in. Having had one look at the patient, she rushes back to the doctor.

Nurse	(*In haste*) Dr Mukherjee!
Doctor	Yes.
Nurse	Patient no. 5 has hemoptysis!
Doctor	Hemoptysis! Why?
Nurse	Why? You please take a look.
Doctor	Let me have a look.

The doctor and the nurse rush into the dormitory.

In the verandah, the queue moves on. Patients receive their medicines and leave one by one.

(*After looking at the patient for a while*) Show me the chart.

The nurse gets the chart.

	(*Checks the chart*) The temperature has risen a great deal. Did you give him the powder?
Nurse	Yes.
Doctor	Ask the Jemadar to get some ice. Quickly.

The doctor starts examining the patient.

Nurse (*Goes towards the verandah*) Jemadar! Jemadar!

Enter Jemadar.

Thora sa baraf lao!

Jemadar	Laata hoon.
Doctor	There's no medicine, no nothing. What the hell!
Nurse	(*Steps forward*) Would you like to give him a glucose injection?
Doctor	We don't have any glucose injection. We don't have any medicines. We only have a room full of patients. It's nonsensical!

The patient at cot no. 5 has a fit. The nurse rushes to him.

Nurse	Dr Mukherjee, patient…
Doctor	I am helpless. There's nothing that I can do.
Nurse	(*Checks pulse*) But doctor, the patient is sinking.
Doctor	(*Screams in English*) Oho! I know Reba he will die. He and the whole lot of them. The future is being murdered, deliberately

murdered! Thieves and bunglers!

The doctor's scream causes all other patients to sit up on their cots. They groan. The chemist peeps in.

>(*Controls himself*) Lie down, lie down all of you. It's nothing. Lie down, all of you lie down. Lie down, yes lie down.

The patients lie down as before, covering themselves with blankets. The nurse hangs a white sheet around the dead patient. Then she goes out to the verandah and stands beside the doctor.

The queue of 'Outdoor' patients has cleared by now. Only the chemist is busy at his desk. Two men enter with a stretcher.

Nurse	(*To the stretcher bearers*) Number five.
A Stretcher Bearer	Ji.

They take dead body out in the stretcher.

Doctor	Yes, it is nonsense, completely false. Forget about your pain. You have no pain.
Pradhan	(*Foolishly*) There's no pain?
Doctor	No. There's no pain. Forget about your pain.
Pradhan	(*He holds on to all the torn clothes, the torn blanket and the rest of the things he is carrying and stands up.*) That is good. Forget it. Forget your pain. You forget about your pain. Forget it.

Exit Pradhan, talking to himself.

The nurse and the doctor look at Pradhan in amazement.

Curtains

Act Four

Scene One

After returning from the city, Niranjan has put in repairs to the house to make it liveable again. As the curtain is pulled aside, a group of about twenty to twenty-five peasants can be seen huddled in the premises of Pradhan Samaddar's house. They are busy deliberating among themselves. There are three groups in the crowd—three to four people in each group—they are standing as they converse. Each group has a unique manner of conducting its discussion. The rest of the peasants sit on the porch. However, their discussion is not as animated as that of the ones standing in the courtyard. The three groups stand out. It is to be noted that as one group talks among themselves, the two other groups stay silent for the convenience of the performance. On the right side of the stage is the first group—Fakir, Sujan and Bhajan. Their discussion starts as soon as the curtain is pulled aside. At the centre and the left side of the stage are the other two groups who are silent or are discussing in inaudible tones. Dayal Mondol, Niranjan and others sit on the porch conversing with each other. As soon as Sakhicharan completes his speech, Barkat calls the gathering to order.

Fakir	(*To Sujan*) I was born with my father's debts. And when I die, my debts will fall on my son's shoulders. This is the way it has always been, for generations. It is not something to be amazed about.
Bhajan	Yes, what you have said is absolutely correct.
Sujan	That is not the way. Just because things have been that way for a long while, does not mean we have to accept it without questioning it. That's not right.
Fakir	What else can be done?
Sujan	We need to find a way.
Fakir	Why hasn't a way been found yet? It is not that the problem has cropped up now.
Sujan	Why hasn't it happened yet? What are you saying, Uncle? If you accept the situation, you will never feel the need for a solution. First, you should recognize it as a problem, isn't it?
Fakir	Yes, that is…
Sujan	See.

With Sujan's speech, the discussion of the first group turns mute and that of the second group becomes audible. The first group continues its conversations but only a few isolated words and gestures can be perceived. The second group consists of Rahim, Barkat and Ghulam Nabi. Barkat carries his little girl—beautifully dressed—on his shoulders.

Rahim	Okay, maybe I can avoid that, but the sacrifice I have to make at the dargha! I cannot avoid it.
Barkat	Why?

Nabanna ▪ 129

Rahim	I had made an oath!
Barkat	I can see you are in great debt.
Ghulam Nabi	If you've made an oath, offer the sacrifice later. There is no harm in doing so. The point is to make an offering. You won't go to hell if you delay it by a few days.
Rahim	But if I do that, the Maulana will not spare me. Already…
Barkat	So what if the Maulana is cross. People may have difficulties. Offer it later if you have to… God is not as narrow-minded as the Maulana, remember that.

With Barkat's speech, the discussion of the second group falls silent. The fourth group's conversations can now be heard—Digambar, Sakhicharan and two others.

Digambar	Arre, I am a debtor to everyone. What can be done about that? I have been repaying debt all my life. I have never got a thing from anyone, ever.
Sakhicharan	If I manage a good harvest this time, let me try to…
Digambar	You are saying that now, but as soon as you have had food, and you are full, you will don your generous self. You will start distributing your produce without discriminating between friend and foe. This is the bane of us peasants—we have hearts like kings but we are paupers by means.
Sakhicharan	No, not this time.

All this while Dayal, Niranjan and others were conversing on the porch. With Sakhicharan's speech, Barkat calls the assembly to order.

Barkat	So Mondol, can we begin our meeting now? I think everyone is here.
Dayal	Yes, why delay any further.
Niranjan	No, there's no need to wait. Let us start the meeting.
Barkat	Yes, let us start.
Digambar	I think everyone is here, now.
Sakhiram	Start the meeting.

Chant of 'Haribol' within.

Barkat   Dayalda, you begin.

He whispers to Niranjan.

Niranjan	Yes. (*Laughs and nods his head.*)
Dayal	Should I begin? Isn't it better that…
Niranjan	No, no, you begin. Speak.
Barkat	You begin, then all of us will join.
Dayal	(*Smiles*) Achha, achha.

Suddenly there is a serious look on Dayal's face. He starts stroking the ground with his fingers. Then he looks up.

The matter is, all of us who have assembled here are very well aware, what the issue is. It is a problem, it is a very serious problem, a matter of life and death—reaping our crops, threshing, storing and protecting them. The situation is so grim that this gathering of ours to discuss this problem that we find ourselves in, is also drawing away precious time when we should

	be working in our fields.
Niranjan	You are right. Very correct.

Chants of 'Haribol' within.

Dayal	I am not denying the need for discussion. There is of course, a great need for it. But conditions demand that we don't waste any time at all. Which is why I made a mention of it. But simply put, if we do not arrive at an arrangement for the protection of our harvest, there shall be no path left for us other than the path to death. We will, all of us, just lie in our houses and die, and no one will be able to do anything about it.

Everyone looks at one another. There is a din of conversations.

	In brief, I have placed the problem before you. Now all of you decide what can be done about it, find the route to a solution. Barkat, you speak.
Barkat	(*Sits up*) What should I say?
Dayal	(Hands him a hookah) Aha! Just tell everyone what you have been thinking about the matter. Everyone is facing this problem.... (*Draws in smoke*)

Chants of 'Haribol' within.

Barkat	What you say is correct.
Niranjan	Tell us what you've been thinking.

Chants of 'Haribol' within grow louder.

Who's died now?

Answer from within—'Trilochan Biswas'.

Digambar	Trilochan—that is Naran's father. Strange! Just the other day I was talking to Naran on the street.
Sakhicharan	What happened to him?
Niranjan	Does it take anything to die?
Barkat	Death has become a usual affair. You can die at will.
Dayal	Yes, complete chaos. But he who has died is now absolved of responsibilities. For those that are left behind, we have to decide the way forward. The paddy has almost ripened. Figure out how you will ensure that it can feed the hungry so that no one dies of starvation.
Fakir	Barkat, complete your point.
Barkat	What more do I have to say?
Digambar	You must say whatever comes to your mind. It need not be the right thing to say. It is only through free-spirited discussion that we will be able to reach a solution to our problem.
Sakhicharan	Yes, everyone should discuss with a free mind.
Barkat	I mean to say that it is not that I have not at all thought about this. I have. But it is not an easy situation, so it is not easy to find a way out of it. Moreover, what is the use of thinking? It is impossible to find someone who can help out. Even if I am willing to pay two or three rupees a day, other than taking care of his food and needs—it is still difficult to find help. How will I ever complete the harvest? And

	there is the overlord, who is threatening that if I don't manage to harvest everything within two days, I will lose whatever remains. Such is the condition. It is not that I haven't thought about it, I have. But that is all. How can my two hands complete the task of twenty men. What more can I say?
Dayal	This is to repeat the problem.
Barkat	Yes, it is. The more I think of it, the more I am unable to figure out what to do, the more I am unable to sleep a wink all night, Mondol. When I get up in the morning I find my face all dried up. My limbs have lost strength.
Digambar	And all the illness around has dampened spirits. The desire to fight it out, do what it takes to survive—where will that desire come from? Where is the human spirit? It is lost.
Dayal	I understand, I can understand; but, Digambar, it is this human spirit which tries to live on. Look at this—there is no help, there are no means, the famine has destroyed all land and property, and yet everyone has come for this meeting, and where? At Niranjan's house, at Niranjan's invitation. How will you stop this? This great desire among people to live on, to fight—how will you resist it?

All fall silent for a while. In a little while, Niranjan clears his throat and through his mannerism tries to show that he has something to say.

Barkat   Do you want to say something, Niranjan? Say it boldly.

Dayal	So Niranjan, do you want to speak? Go on, say what you have to say.
Niranjan	No, I was simply saying…
Dayal	Yes…
Niranjan	No, I was merely saying…
Dayal	Yes…
Niranjan	What Barkat Chacha and Digambarda were speaking of—all the disease and sadness that has enveloped our lives—that has in a sense become a part of our lives. It is not that if we sit together and talk about it there will be any remedy to that.
Dayal	Right.
Niranjan	If we have to do anything, we have to find a way out of these very conditions.
Digambar	Everyone has understood that, that we have to do something. But 'what is to be done', that is where we are all stuck. What is to be done?
Barkat	That is the crucial point. Achha…
Dayal	Continue, say what you have to say.
Barkat	I was saying that if the Jamidar Babu… all Jamidars… the payment of rent for the last few years…
Dayal	Should be waived?
Barkat	Yes.
Dayal	Fine. Go on petitioning—rent should be waived, seeds should be provided, farming loans should be provided—these demands are there. But my point is that instead of relying completely on the authorities, if there is something that we can do by ourselves, whatever we can do.

Nabanna ▪ 135

Digambar	Yes, we must not adopt the chatak bird's[104] strategy from the very beginning and wait for things to trickle down. That would be no good.
Sakhicharan	Yes.
Manik	No, that would only bring false hope.
Dayal	Why don't we do something!

Everyone looks on anxiously.

All of you should consider it carefully.

There are shouts of—'What do you mean? What are you trying to tell us?' etc.

I am saying, why don't we work for each other?

Barkat	Work for each other!
Dayal	Yes. Let's take Aminpur as an example. At least forty to fifty householders live here. We would probably not be able to get all the households together for work, for there can be illnesses and mourning, or other unforeseen situations. But even if we get the help of half the households, let's say about twenty-five and if we pledge to work together in each other's land, I firmly believe that not a grain would go waste. If we work together we will be able to harvest everything.

Everyone in the gathering look at each other. From their expressions, it seems that they support Dayal's idea.

Digambar	(*Nods his head*) Yes, it can be done.
Sakhicharan	His logic is correct.

Sujan	If we put our minds and hearts together and work for each other we would manage.
Ghulam Nabi	Absolutely, what he is saying makes a lot of sense.
Fakir	This way we may be able to complete the harvest. But...
Dayal	Mian, that would be no small matter.
Fakir	Yes, the harvesting would be done. But that is not the end to our woes. It's not about who will protect but about how we will protect it—from the jamidar[105], the mahajan[106], the guards...
Dayal	He will come to that. He'll talk of these problems.
Sujan	Yes. The rent's been pending for a long while. And all of us owe a lot of money to the mahajan as well. The moment we stock up our harvest will all the vultures will swarm in immediately—'pay rent, pay rent, pay rent'.
Dayal	We have to prevent that somehow. First the rent-payer has to survive.
Sujan	No one will listen to that.
Dayal	We have to make them listen. We can't just let things be.
Barkat	Yes, we have to plan accordingly. Now we should organize everything.
Dayal	First of all we must ensure that the crops don't go wasted.
Sujan	Absolutely.
Dayal	Right. So let us talk about one thing at a time.
Digambar	What is everyone's opinion on working for

each other? Is everyone willing to work for each other? Speak with a clear mind.

All in unison, 'Yes of course', 'We will work for each other'.

Barkat Yes, let us complete the harvest. Whatever hurdles come in our way, we cannot foresee everything. We can deal with them if we stick together.

Dayal (*Joining in*) We shall be able to find a way out of it.

Digambar The main object is the harvest. (*In joy*) If we are able to secure the entire harvest I will give away half of my produce to the poor peasant families.

Budhe (*A dim-witted peasant*) I will give away all my produce. I won't keep even a bit of what my four bighas produce.

Dayal (*Laughs*) If you give away everything, what will you eat and how will you survive! Dhoosh!

Everyone laughs.

Fakir Whose produce are we talking of? He has already sold his land. How can he give away the grains from that land? Do the grains belong to him? And…

Ghulam Nabi There's a point there.

Barkat Yes, these problems are all there. All right, let us settle at that for now and then meet at Dayal Mondol's place in the evening. Be there on time all of you.

Dayal (*Stands up*) Yes, such problems will always be

there. But right now, we need to start cutting the rice, from tomorrow morning. We can't afford to wait.

Everyone gets up, folds their gamchhas and cotton shawls, places them on the shoulders and slowly exits the stage from the left and the right.

Dayal	(*Gets off the porch, spots Barkat's daughter and walks up to her.*) Who's that? Who's that?
Niranjan	(With a smile) She is Barkat Chacha's daughter. Very shy.
Dayal	Oh really! (*Moves up*) Is it true? Are you very shy? (*Places his hand on the head of Barkat's daughter*) Wouldn't she be shy? She has been tied in a nikah with me, isn't it?
Barkat's daughter	Jah! (*Hides her face in Barkat's lap*)
Dayal	Okay, now look at me carefully and see if you like me. What do you say? Will you marry me?

The girl catches hold of Dayal's beard in a flash.

Uh! Uh! Let me go! (*Frees himself*) What a tyrant of a wife, baap re, what a tyrant of a wife!

Everyone laughs. The girl giggles. Exit all, except Fakir, Niranjan, Barkat and Barkat's daughter.

Fakir Hoon! Work for each other. Will working for each other solve all problems? What about lands that have been transferred, what is the use of working on those lands? And those who have taken a loan against their produce—what about their land? What is the point of working

	on their land? The Jotedar and the Mahajan will enjoy the fruits of our labour.
Barkat	All those difficulties are there. No one is denying…
Fakir	What will we get out of this?
Barkat	Should we not make an effort? Should we just be idle?
Fakir	Fine then! Make your effort.

Exit Fakir.

Barkat	This Fakir is a strange kind of man!
Niranjan	(*Sits on the porch, preparing tobacco*) Why are you standing, Barkat Chacha? Sit down.
Barkat	Yes, yes, let me sit.
Niranjan	(*Blows the hookah*) Is he human? Barkat Chacha, could you ever imagine that you would return to your own land, that you would start living here again, that you would once again…

Looks on at Barkat.

Barkat	(*Smoking his hookah*) This is how time moves. In waves, in highs and lows, highs and lows…
Niranjan	(*Nods*) Right, right! Barkat Chacha, at times I get the feeling that the boat won't move anymore, it is stuck in the shallows. But then I find that it has begun moving again, running along the stream. The shallows have been left behind. Strange, very strange.
Barkat	This is the way of the world. (*The two of them sit silently for a while.*) It is late, Niranjan, I'll

	leave now. (*Gets up*)
Niranjan	Achha. I hope you will be there at Mondol's place?
Barkat	Yes, you must come as well.

Moves towards the exit.

Niranjan	(*Follows him to the exit*) Sure, I'll come.

Exit Barkat.

Niranjan moves to the porch and lies down. Binodini lights a kerosene lamp on the porch and then on one end of the courtyard, lights a fire to cook rice in an earthen pot. In dim light, the flame dances around the pot. Niranjan sings.

> Tough times, trying times,
> > Would get us gold,
> Those wise words have failed,
> > I am helpless.
> The fire of hardship, and glory of happy times,
> > The wise men speak of,
> I heard of this wisdom,
> > From a bard on the road.
> > I am helpless.

As the song ends, enter Kunja and Radhika.

Kunja	(*In a tired voice*) Who knows whose house this is? (*Sighs*) Oh God!
Radhika	(*In a weak voice*) I can't make out anything in the darkness.
Niranjan	(*Sits up hurriedly*) Who's there? Who speaks there?

Kunja	(*Rattled*) Here, it is us.
Niranjan	(*Stands up*) 'Us'? Who's 'us'?
Kunja	We. Achha, can you tell us the way to Pradhan Samaddar's house?
Niranjan	Pradhan Samaddar? (*Takes a few steps in astonishment*) This is Pradhan Samaddar's house, but who are you?
Kunja	We! (*Looks at Radhika*) Niranjan, doesn't he look like Niranjan?
Niranjan	Wait. Can you get the light, my dear?

Binodini comes forward with the kerosene lamp. All faces light up in the red glow of the lamp. They keep looking at each other for a moment.

Dada, is that you?

Binodini hugs Radhika.

Kunja	(*In a hoarse voice*) This is our Niranjan. The same Niranjan. (*Suddenly*) Come, show me your head... I had hit you on the head... show me. (*Passes his hand over Niranjan's forehead*) It doesn't hurt, does it?
Niranjan	(*Overwhelmed*) No.

They embrace each other.

Kunja	This is our Niranjan.

Kunja draws Niranjan's head towards his chest.

Curtains

Scene Two

Kunja's household. The open space has filled up with freshly harvested crops. On one side of the courtyard Niranjan threshes rice against a high bamboo frame. He wears a gamchha around his head. There is a heap of grains on the ground below. Radhika fills the grains into a wicker basket. On the left side of the courtyard, a large store of grain can be seen. A man, with gamchha tied around his head, picks up grains—one bunch at a time—and hands them to Niranjan. Another man threshes grains alongside Niranjan. Binodini winnows the grains. Kunja walks up and down the courtyard with a hookah in his hand. Everyone is busy working hard in the bright daylight. They all seem to be alive after a long time. Having filled up half her basket, Binodini cracks a joke with Radhika and almost rolls in laughter. Radhika laughs silently as she holds the grain-filled winnowing fork above her head. Niranjan finishes threshing a few more bunches of grain and then falls, exhausted, on the heap of straw. He wipes sweat off his forehead and turns to Binodini.

Niranjan   (*To Binodini, who is still smiling*) Look at them! Just look at them! They are just rolling about, having fun. You are doing a good job of winnowing the rice. If we go on like this...

Binodini laughs even more. She falls headlong on the grains.

O ma! Have you seen her? (*In a false show of rage*) Boudi,[107] why won't you tell her anything?

In response, Radhika's laughter increases. The winnowing fork almost falls off her hands.

Nabanna ▪ 143

	You too! What has taken over all of you?
Binodini	(*Controlling her laughter*) I have seen a horse's wings.

Radhika laughs.

Niranjan	(*Takes up a few more bunches of the harvested crops*) It seems so.

Threshing.

Radhika	(*Stops laughing. Fills up a winnowing fan with rice and hands it to Binodini*) Get up! And get to work. Too much laughter is no good. (*Laughs and points towards Niranjan*) Wise people say the more you laugh, the more you have to cry.

Winnowing.

Niranjan	(*To Radhika*) There comes the 'wise man', he will see you laughing. (*Radhika gets back to work. Binodini covers her head with the anchal*) Why did you stop laughing?

Threshing.

Kunja	(*Advances towards Radhika*) Do we have enough rice for eleven katthas[108]? Put it in. (*Pleased with himself*) Let mine be the first to go to the common barn.
Radhika	Why eleven, when we had decided it would be ten?
Niranjan	Ten. Yes, that is what we had decided at Mondolda's house.

Kunja	Ten katthas? Fine, I will add one more kattha from my share. When I've said eleven, let it be eleven.
Niranjan	(*Pleased*) You decide that. Give more if you so desire. After all, it will go to the common barn.

Enter Dayal.

Dayal	What are your sending to the common barn?

Radhika and Binodini cover their heads.

Kunja	Oh! Mondol you've come. We were talking of rice. I was telling them that my share of rice should be the first to go into the common barn.
Dayal	(*Laughs and moves his hand over his bald head*) Good, very good. So have you finished preparing the rice?
Kunja	It is almost done.
Dayal	Good. (*To Radhika with a smile*) Now you should prepare pithe[109] with the new rice for all of us.
Kunja	(*Laughs*) Yes, that is a must. Nabanna is here.
Niranjan	Achha Mondolda, won't we celebrate Nabanna this time?
Dayal	Nabanna festival—of course! We must. We must celebrate.
Niranjan	(*Laughs*) Just like we do every year. This year too we will celebrate it. There will be games and we shall play with sticks.
Dayal	Yes, this time I shall have a match with you. Be prepared.
Niranjan	(*Laughs*) With me, achha, achha.
Dayal	(*Smiles*) With bamboo sticks.

Niranjan	Fine, as you wish.
Dayal	And if you lose?
Niranjan	(*With enthusiasm*) Then I will feed you one seer of jilipi[110].
Dayal	(*To Kunja and the rest*) Did you hear what he said? He will feed me one seer jilipi, if he loses. (*To Niranjan*) Remember what you said.

Moves to exit.

Niranjan	(*Laughs*) Yes, yes, I'll remember. One seer is not much.
Kunja	Mondolda, are you leaving?
Dayal	Yes, I want to go by the fields... its Barkat's turn today, isn't it?
Kunja	Yes. You go ahead, I'll join you.

Exit Dayal.

Niranjan	(*Laughs. Almost choking*) Oof! Mondolda is...
Radhika	(*Uncovers her head*) Even though he is old, Mondolda has a lot of zest.
Binodini	(*Laughs*) Mondolda is good with the stick. You accepted the challenge, but take care not to lose your face in front of the entire village.
Niranjan	Aah! You let it be. I have seen many a Mondol.
Radhika	(*Teasing Niranjan*) Be prepared to part with one seer of jilipi.
Kunja	Come on, have you finished preparing rice worth eleven katthas? If you while away your time in laughing and talking, when will you manage to finish the work?
Radhika	(*Makes a show of rage*) Who's stopping you?

146 ▪ *Bijon Bhattacharya*

	Go ahead and fill the common barn. What calamity? I'll go deaf if I have to go on listening to 'eleven kattha', 'eleven kattha'.
Niranjan	It's ready, why don't you take it?
Radhika	Bino, fill rice in the kattha.
Kunja	Dear wife, the rice is meant for the common barn, don't regret giving it away. Remember the time…
Radhika	O ma! Why should I regret it. The rice is going to the common barn, why should…here, take this.

Radhika keeps the winnowing fan on the ground. She takes the wicker basket from Binodini and hands it over to Kunja. Kunja transfers the grains to the barn. Niranjan continues to thresh the grains. Binodini fills up another wicker basket with grains.

Kunja	(*Transferring grains to the barn*) The rice belongs to someone and someone else gives it away. Such a heartburn was created over the sale of this land, ooh! What a life—we did not even meet for one last time. Who knows where he maybe? He may be dead by now. Anyway, let me do my work.
Radhika	(*Carrying the second wicker basket*) Here, hold this.
Kunja	Oh! Here, you take this.

Radhika takes the empty basket from Kunja and gives it to Binodini.

Radhika   Here…

Enter a fakir wearing a loose shirt. With a whisk in hand, he begins to sing. Behind him two fakirs sing as chorus—'Your name lives on if you are alive.'

Fakir (*Let's out a cry and then keeps muttering*) O-o-o
(*mutters again*)
It isn't true that the family name survives only with you,
All peasants must join hands—be it Muslim or Hindu.
There is no other way now, all should know,
If we haven't learnt our lesson yet, will we ever do?
(Now) those who knowingly stay alone and apart,
Beyond six months they cannot last.
Jabbar of Khalilpur—you must know of his pain.
Hostility with his neighbour was his bane.
Countless are peasants who have agonized,
Before their time many have died.
The death of our cattle, no one kept a count,
Dead women and children to lakhs may amount.
Some women have themselves been forced to sell,
They found no help in times of hell.
Infants suck in vain at their mothers' dead breasts,
Before they saw life, their birth was a waste.
No clothes, no robes, nothing to wear,
Skin, bones, viscera, all things bare.
Ershad's wife in Kalshikathi had no wraps,
They stole shrouds from a dug up corpse.
In every house there is the living dead,

                Every home has hunger visited.
                Fields full of rice and eyes full of tears,
                But have full faith on the plough and the shears.
                Hold on to the plough, it will produce gold.
                Selfish desires and pride is all a farce,
                You must be strong and bold in your hearts.
                The winter harvest is a blessing for all,
                Reap the grain together, one and all.
                For selfish goals, you should not suffer,
                This is all this humble fakir has to offer.

Refrain by all   The family name survives…join hands.

At the end of the song, Radhika uses a small basket to pour some rice into the fakir's satchel.

Curtains

Scene Three

A dry river bank, a wide expansive scape. The sun is about to set. The setting sun lights up the sky in red. The entire landscape is coloured in the reddish tinge. Today is the Nabanna festival, which is why the old and young of the village have thronged the river bank. Many of the figures are lean and malnourished, a reminder of the famine that has just gone by. Yet there are preparations for the festival this evening. Peasants are participating in the festivities with tremendous enthusiasm and energy. All the characters—peasant householders— who participated in the action in Act One, Scene One, are present here in different attires. Most of them are bare bodied, and carry a gamchha each—wearing it either around their head or waist, or carrying it over their shoulder.

Cattle moo within. The bells around the cattle can be heard. Sounds of drums can be heard intermittently.

The curtain rises. A four-feet-high wall meant for shadow play. Women sit in front of the wall singing and chewing betel leaves. Their hair glisten in the light. People present are engaged in laughter and conversation.

Front stage—peasants sit with fighter roosters in their laps. The roosters have strings tied to their feet and they flutter their wings once in a while. As the women finish their song, the fight begins. The crowd gathers around it. The roosters fight in doubles. The owner of the winning pair is presented with a gamchha and a sickle.

The fight is followed by a peasants' song, after which there is a cattle race. Sounds of running cattle within. This scene will have to be staged through a shadow play. Alternatively it can also be screened using cardboard cutouts of cattle or with puppets. The bells around the necks of the bulls should ring vigorously and there should be a loud sound of the cows running within. The owner of the winning bull would be presented with a new dhoti and a new plough.

As the cattle race finishes, there is the clamour of drums and cymbals. It is time for the stick fight to begin. It begins with sticks and cane-shields. The players move in rhythm with the drum beats. After a couple of rounds, at the beginning of the third round, Pradhan appears.

(The peasant women sing).

Downcast eyes and necklace adorn her
Her wide bordered saree and santhali garland
She walks the dyke in fresh marriage hues
Smile and move on, don't say a word.

During the song, eight men sit with eight roosters in two rows of four each. The roosters' feet have strings attached to the left hand index fingers of each of the eight men; they can't fly away. Each man is praising the roosters they own, patting them on their heads. When the song ends, conversations resume.

1st man in 1st row (*Restrains the rooster he owns as it tries to fly away*) Arre! Arre! Byata! He can't wait for the fight.

2nd man in 2nd row (*As his rooster flaps its wings*) O man! O man! O man! His temper has risen with all the talk. Just watch him, he is raring to go. Yes, yes, you will fight, wait a bit.

2nd man in 3rd row (*With the rooster in his lap*) I could not get hold of the bigger one. Just when I tried to catch it, it ran into the forest. (*To the rooster*) I could get hold of this one, so brought him here. Though he is a bit weak, he has a good technique. He is very good with his trapping. Even the bigger one does not dare come close to him.

1st man in 2nd row (*To the 2nd man in 1st row*) Mian, why have you got that baby chick? There are only sturdy, strong roosters here. It doesn't stand a chance!

2nd man in 1st row (*Smiles*) Which baby?

1st man in 2nd row I am talking of the rooster in your lap. Why didn't you get a better one?

2nd man in 1st row (*With a contemptuous laugh*) You can say that!

3rd man in 1st row (*To the 1st man in 2nd row*) Do you even know what you are saying? Do you know where that rooster is from?

1st man in 2nd row (*Taken aback*) Where from?

2nd man in 1st row (*To the 3rd man in the 1st row*) Let it be. Let him say what he wants to.

3rd man in 1st row That rooster may look small—such is its species. But it can bite.

2nd man in 1st row It has defeated larger roosters in three blows flat. You have no idea of its calibre, so you call it a 'baby'!

3rd man in 1st row (*Touches the beak of the rooster in the lap of the 2nd man in 1st row*) Just check its beak. As hard as a stone. It doesn't strike, it cuts.

The rooster crows.

1st man in 2nd row (*Dejected*) It's my turn now.

2nd man in 1st row I knew it as soon as I saw it. It can't do much if it survives on rice.

1st man in 2nd row True.

Dayal Why are you still seated with the roosters in your laps? Get started!

1st man in 1st row Yes, we can start as soon as the judges are here.

Dayal Judges? I think all judges are here. (*Calls out*) O Kunja, come up here with Barkat Mian. Let's get going with the rooster fight. (*To the contestants*) Come on, get started now.

(*Looks at the roosters*) I see we have a good set of roosters this time.

The judges and the crowd stand behind the two rows of men. In the middle, the roosters fight in pairs. The spectators egg on the roosters. The sound of women singing along with the sound of anklets can be heard from within. Within two or three minutes, the rooster fights are over. The 4th man in the 2nd row wins the competition. He is held up by the others.

Kunja (*Announces with a smile on his face*) Feku Mian—for being the winner of the rooster fight, we are presenting Feku Mian with a gamchha and a sickle.

Feku Mian receives the prize with a smile on his face. Once again, he is held aloft by others amidst loud cheers.

Feku Mian (*Smiling*) Be careful! What are you doing? I'll fall.

Everyone sings.

> (Aha!) Feku mian's rooster has won.
> Feku mian's beard is bloated boastfully
> (Aha!) Feku Mian's rooster has won.

After repeating the lines a few times, the crowd thins out. They run upstage in a hurry. Sounds of cattle running and the ringing of bells within. Shadow play technique can be used to project three or four bulls onto the back curtain. The tails of two of the bulls in the shadow can be raised to indicate speed. There should be constant sound of commotion and running within. In the midst of it all, cattle can be heard mooing. In a little while the crowd enters the stage holding up a peasant.

Cries of 'Who won? Who won?' within.

Someone among those on stage answers back—'Rahmatullah'.

The crowd dances about having lifted Rahmatullah on their shoulders.

Kunja (*Raises his voice amidst the din*) This year

the quality of cattle has been poor compared to the kind of cattle that usually comes for this event each year. For most of the bullocks have died and those that are left have been severely weakened in the famine. Initially, we had decided that the cattle race would be cancelled this year. But then at Mondol's insistence, we decided to have it. Mondol said that cattle is the life centre of this festival of ours. So, even if they are weak, we must have the cattle race. The bulls do not have strength, so the cattle race has not been too exciting this time. Nevertheless, the number of quality bulls has not been altogether negligible. And it was Rahmatullah's bull that won the race. So Rahmat bhai would be presented with a new dhoti and a plough. The plough has been presented by Dayal Mondol.

Dayal There must be strong and quality cattle next time.

Rahmat glistens in pride and the crowd cheers him.

Kunja You must make them all plough well this time.

Immediately, the sound of drums and cymbals playing within can be heard. The music has a rhythm. It is time for the stick fight. The drummers and the cymbal-players enter the stage and start going around the edges while playing their instruments. Two men wearing red loin cloth stand at the centre with sticks in their right hands and shields made of cane in their left. They start the fight on the rhythm of the music. The first round comes to an end with three drum beats. Two fresh players enter the arena for the second round. Once again, the beats are heard. This pair plays in style. After the second round, two old men engage in stick fight for the third round. The play begins at a slow pace. In a little while, Pradhan can be seen approaching the arena. He walks in rhythm. Sound of thunder within.

1st Spectator The northern sky is clouded. Come on, let us finish this quickly.

No one listens to him. The fight gathers pace as the tempo of the music rises. Suddenly some people in the crowd spot Pradhan. They look at each other as if they are unable to recognize the man. Pradhan makes some sounds as he advances towards the crowd. Suddenly, a member of the crowd shouts out. Sounds of thunder.

2nd Spectator (*Shouting at the top of his voice*) Morol[111], Morol, Morol has come! Morol!

Pradhan advances while nodding his head. He carries the lot of rubbish on him as before. Everyone looks at him. The crowd moves to one side. The music stops.

Pradhan I have come. I have arrived.

Among the crowd stands Dayal ready for the stick fight, wearing a red loin cloth. His eyes are filled with tears of joy. He is unable to speak. Kunja and Niranjan too, are mute.

I have come. I have come.

A black cloud covers the sky.

Dayal (*In a state of disbelief, speaks in a very low voice*) Pradhan, have you come? Pradhan, Pradhan…
Kunja (*Shouts out in joy and embraces Pradhan*) Jetha!

	Jetha! Jetha!
Pradhan	(*As if trying to remember*) Is this Kunja? My Kunja?

He examines Kunja's face with his hands.

	Kunja, Kunja. (*Sounds of thunder*)
Dayal	(*Advances*) Pradhan, can you recognize this old man. Ha! Can you recognize me!

Pradhan's face is almost hidden behind his long beard and dishevelled hair. But even through that cover one can see his face lighting up.

Pradhan	(*Raising his index finger*) You, you are Baburali. (*Dayal stands beside him like a statue*) Yes, yes, you are Kripanath.

Dayal stays silent.

	You… you… who are you?
	(*Laughing out*) Dayal! Dayal! You are Dayal!
Dayal	Yes, do you remember, Pradhan?
Pradhan	(*Laughs as he raises his index finger*) Yes, I can remember. Dayal, you are Dayal.

Pradhan weeps.

Sounds of thunder.

Dayal	Today is the Nabanna festival.
Pradhan	Nabanna festival. Good, very good, Nabanna festival. Good days have returned. The dark days have gone by. The dark days are over. They won't return again.
Dayal	What fear do we have even if they return?
Pradhan	There's no fear. No fear of difficult times. Good,

	very good, very good.
Dayal	There may be fear, Pradhan, but we have faced the famine. We did not perish. We are alive. Here we are, all of us—Kunja, Niranjan, Barkat, Sakhicharan. Do you remember all of them? The famine could not kill us.
Pradhan	No we did not die. We did not die. Good, good. But Dayal, what if the famine returns? If the famine comes again?

Sounds of thunder. One fourth of the festival area is darkened by a cloud.

> (*Indicating the cloud*) Look here. Here on the ground we are celebrating, we are happy, and there, right there a big trouble is looming over us. A big, dark trouble. A huge…

He shakes his head with a frown.

Dayal I know, Pradhan, that there are apprehensions in your mind. But keep this in mind that unlike the last time, the difficult times will not be able to creep in and snatch away my relations, friends; (*pointing towards the crowd*) here, all you are my friends and family. No, never again. If it wants to harm them, first it will have to face me, kill me. It will have to overthrow our solidarity. Only then it may succeed. There will be great resistance the next time. Great resistance. A great resistance.

Pradhan (*Shouts out loud as he embraces Dayal*) Dayal!

Curtains

Production Note for *Nabanna*[112]

Bijon Bhattacharya

Perhaps no poetry can be born without emotions—in the absence of feelings or pain, no creativity is possible. As I try to look back at the production of *Nabanna* after twenty-five years, these are the thoughts that keep returning to me. When *Nabanna* was produced, I had written the play with the country in my mind, not being influenced by any party or a specific ideology. Though my party did not stand in support of the August movement of 1942, I had felt a tremendous enthusiasm for it. It frightens me to think how I came face to face with grave danger on many occasions. So many people fell beside me when the bullets were fired—that it wasn't me, was just an accident. Then the cries filled up the streets of Calcutta—that tide of the hungry multitudes was there before us. This picture of suffering made life unbearable for me. At home I used to shut the doors during meals—it was impossible to swallow the food. There was this constant urge, that something had to be done about it. The mute cries of anguish from the streets made me restless. At that time, I was young, my body had unlimited strength, and my dreams were limitless. Anyway, the IPTA had decided to produce this play. Even earlier, two plays had been produced, but *Nabanna* was perhaps the first milestone. Everyone in the group was fired together by an inspiration. Not to become stars, but to work together—to produce the play. *Nabanna* was not produced only by actors or artists. Inputs from other activists, efforts by many others, encouragement by the Progressive Writers Association—we must remember all contributions in one thread. The 'Party' got involved in the search for female actors. Among those who came were a few who had never considered taking up a career on stage. Some of the girls who joined the production had never previously stepped beyond the domestic boundary. For instance, Sova Sen. There were some who were known for activities other than the theatre, such as Manikuntala Sen, Kalyani Kumaramangalam, famed actors of the contemporary stage—Shombhu Mitra, Tripti Bhaduri (Mitra), Charuprakash Ghosh, Sajal Roychowdhury, Sudhi Pradhan, Gangapada Basu and others. In this context it must be noted that Manidi[113] (Manikuntala Sen) was initially reluctant to act as she had never been on stage before. But I explained to her—Manidi, only you can play Matangini Hazra on stage because playing her character requires a certain political insight which as a political activist you have—not all actors have such insight. Several actors have performed the role of Matangini— but I distinctly remember the depth in Manidi's portrayal of the character.

Maharshi Manaranjan Bhattacharya advised us to use jute cloth to create the scenic design. Once during a performance of *Nabanna* at Srirangam (now Biswarupa), Maharshi called out to me, 'Bijon come here for a moment, I have to tell you something.' When I went to him he said, 'A member of the audience just came up to me to congratulate me on the achievement of my son. I did not tell him that you are not my son. Just take care, not to spill the truth.' At this, I told him in a choked voice, 'They are not wrong. You are like a father to me.' Maharshi had assisted us in every possible way. We had to toil a lot for police permission. Instead of the sound of gunfire, I had included the sound of the clash of bamboo sticks. We told the police that it was the sound of burnt bamboo sticks, but what we really meant them to stand for was the sound of gunfire—the audience understood, but the police did not.

I can remember a few more names. Many of them are no longer alive. There was the writer Swarnakamal Bhattacharya. The realistic depiction of a beggar which he put up using his thin body is unforgettable. Today he is not amongst us but we can never forget his performance. In today's event Satyajibon Bhattacharya and Gyan Majumdar are present. Anyway, with everyone engaged we were involved in the production with exceptional enthusiasm.

We received unprecedented success. Those who are opposed to us carried out a defamation campaign. In one of the shows some people threw rotten tomatoes and eggs at the actors. I thought this is not a play for any particular party, in this play we are talking about the people, we are presenting the picture of the villages, and they are bhadraloks, why are you behaving like this? Such attacks only strengthened our resolve. And that resolve does help overcome all the insults. Not only in Bengal, *Nabanno* is a stir across India.

But today when we take stock of that moment twenty-five years later, I don't feel the same enthusiasm. Not even in this felicitation ceremony. Perhaps *Nabanna* does not inspire us anymore. If it did, there would not have been such a poverty of culture everywhere around us. Just look at the office clubs. For a night's entertainment they spend up to ten or twelve thousand rupees. It's a luxurious affair. Some clubs hire female entertainers and that is followed by sensuous parties and feasts. Instead, if the real purpose was springtime entertainment the clubs could have hired theatre groups and paid them some five hundred or seven hundred rupees. It might save the clubs some money but it would be a lifeline for the theatre groups. The theatre groups are in a desperate situation today. *And what are some of the plays being performed today*—though they were very relevant in their own time. We need new plays today, which is why, according to me, real consciousness for the theatre is non-existent today. If such consciousness existed, theatre groups would not have been where they are. People in the theatre have lost touch with theatre movement. They are unable to produce any original thought on cultural issues. Lack of consciousness is understandable. The Congress government even created the popular entertainment division. But I don't think it does any work of any value. We will have to work among the people in the villages in a sustained manner. If the effort is not sustained, the people of the villages will doubt the commitment of the actors. Till such time that we can raise the consciousness of people and the artists, it is not possible to create a robust and relevant literature. In the villages across Bengal there are many groups whose names most of us have never heard. In Burdwan or Bankura there is the 'alkap'. In the Bengal–Bihar border area there is Nautanki. Forms like these are the staples for these groups. The way these artists can inform themselves about the lives of the rural people, the way they can mingle with their audiences, cannot be matched by artists from the cities who travel across to perform in the villages. This is why I think, in

Bengal, without an effective cultural movement, real political change will never come about. Due to this error the Congress did not manage to achieve much and if they repeat it, even the United Front will not be any different. They are all busy in the procurement of rice grains. But what they do not understand is that before the procurement of rice is a greater need for the procurement of hearts. And those of you who are enlightened members of the audience, why would you not rise up against our culture which tries to push films filled with cheap gags and song sequences and pass them off as entertainment? It is you who will have to take up the responsibility of creating a healthy and enlightened cultural practice. We should not give in to any posturing or be misled by deception and be always vigilant of hypocrisy—only then can we say that we have lived up to the inheritance of *Nabanna*.

Nabanna and Me[114]

Sova Sen

In Bengal, the people's theatre movement began at a moment of political crisis. This was also a period of greatest crisis during the Second World War. We felt the effects of the crisis in Bengal as well. There was a mood of despondency across the province due to the famine of 1943. There was a corresponding crisis in the cultural field in Bengal, that is, it was affected by the turmoil in the political and social life. It was right at that moment that the IPTA was born through the efforts of a team of progressive young people.

The booklet published on the occasion of the first performance of *Nabanna* noted, 'the Bengali theatres are unable to meet the needs of their audiences. The forces of contradiction in contemporary society had disturbed the peace of the people. The IPTA built up its heritage in the struggle amidst these contradictions. This is why the emergence of the people's theatre movement in Bengal was a historic occasion. The task of the IPTA is to enliven the sphere of cultural practice and link it to the wider experiences of the people.

This linkage will enrich culture and civilization. The role of culture in strengthening the revolutionary energies of the people is unquestionable. That is why the IPTA is leading the cultural movement in the country with a great degree of Patriotism.

Earlier, political parties would consider culture to be a thing which was not linked to the struggles in the political arena. For them culture was an object of fun, fit to be watched from a distance. The heritage of Mukunda Das or the idea of the people's theatre and people's culture weren't borne by urban intellectuals or the 'babu' culture. In fact, those who initiated the people's cultural movement in the very early years did not fathom the full implications of this movement. But when the famine came, when hunger hit the skies, it was then that a few artists and political activists came together. They were searching for ways in which they could generate funds from the public. Towards this goal, in 1940, the Youth Cultural Institute was set up. They made cultural tours with short plays and songs.

That period was witness to the Shishir era on the Bengali stage coming to an end. Professional stage had lost its connection with the audiences. They could neither satisfy the audiences with older themes and ideas any longer, nor could they put up any plays of a newer kind. Moreover, the theatre owners refused to change their attitudes to make way for a new form of theatre.

It was around this time, in 1942, that the IPTA emerged as the dramatics section of the Anti-Fascist Writers, and Artists, Association. Bengal was being ravaged by famine, malnutrition, drought and war. Human lives were at stake. Which is why even for cultural organizations it became imperative to undertake a campaign to save Bengal. So the IPTA joined the countrywide mass movement against famine and hunger. Small groups of artists spread across the country with songs, dances and plays to collect relief contributions. The cultural action managed to overcome barriers of language and regionalism. The energy produced by the IPTA movement attracted the youth from across India.

Even I could not resist the temptation to join that movement. Like me, many other youths too joined the IPTA. The Communist Party became their torchbearer. The IPTA functioned as a democratic front of the Communist Party. Thus there were many artists who may not have been convinced by the call for socialism, but felt welcome in the IPTA. They worked alongside other artists who did adopt socialism as their goal. A certain section of artists also joined the IPTA with humanist ideals alone. In the IPTA, communist and non-communist artists shared the common goal of working for the people. Across the country they created a culture which was of the people, by the people, and for the people. There were some artists who joined simply because their friends had. Whatever the attraction may have been, all artists became inspired by a spirit of patriotism. It was of immense benefit for the common good.

Rehearsals for *Nabanna* commenced in Calcutta. The year was 1944. The venue was a medium-sized room on the second floor of a building in Harrison Road. Shri Bijon Bhattacharya and Shri Shombhu Mitra were jointly in charge of direction. Sudhi Pradhan and then secretary Shri Chitta Banerjee were in charge of production. It was Sudhibabu who took me to Bijonbabu one day. Bijonbabu asked me to read from an extract of *Nabanna* which had been published in *Arani*. He passed me in the test and instructed me to appear for rehearsals regularly. I enjoyed the rehearsals. Till then I had never thought that I would be an actor, though I did have an interest in acting during my childhood. But that interest turned into a passion till acting ultimately became my profession—a journey which amazes me.

The rehearsals went on for nearly four months. I used to travel from Goabagan. Tripti used to live with her sister. Tripti had cleared her matriculation and had entered the intermediary level. I had just completed my graduation. Tripti and I were to perform the principal female characters in the play. Me as Radhika and Tripti as Binodini. Bijonda used to train us as actors. We used to follow his instructions with great care. This was my first experience on stage, so I was quite nervous. Tripti had performed in *Jabanbandi* and had earned a name for herself. So she was not too nervous. I was new and my character was complex. She belonged to a poor peasant household. On the one hand her child was hungry, and on the other her home was being destroyed completely. The agony was unimaginable. I was anxious about being able to portray this mental agony on stage. But the character was very lifelike. I considered myself very fortunate to have been given that role. I tried my best to understand the character. I had a strong voice which is why both directors had chosen me. And they worked hard to prepare me for the performance. Whatever success I may have achieved in life, the contribution of the two directors of *Nabanna* has been the greatest. I shall always remain grateful to them.

We were all extremely anxious about *Nabanna*. Few people felt the IPTA comprised of a set of mad people and they were extremely suspicious of the group's activities. The IPTA had hired the Srirangam Theatre for a week. We were anxious as well. So we put our mind and body into the rehearsals. On the rehearsal floor the entire team of actors had become a single family. Every evening we would be drawn by passion to that room on Harrison Road. The rehearsals stretched to nine, sometimes till ten in the night. Bijonda used to teach us the dialect of the peasants of Medinipore. So we used to reach the rehearsal space a little early each evening. Bijonda and Shambhubabu used to live there. Sometimes, Bijonda found time to go home. Bijonda trained us in acting. And Shambhubabu used to train a group of boys in stage techniques. Together they devised a stage created from jute fabric—a fact now known to many.

The first round of performances of *Nabanna* took place at Srirangam Theatre in October–November 1944. The first night is always a mixture of anticipation and apprehensions. It is a test all artists have to face. We waited with baited breath and made-up faces. We were instructed to do our make-up ourselves. We had, therefore, learnt the make-up techniques from our elders, and improvized a little. The time for performance neared. Almost everyone was nervous. Everyone was determined to put up a good performance. We all felt that this was our duty towards our country, towards the people.

The curtain was raised. The first scene commenced. It depicted a peasant struggle during the Quit India Movement of 1942. It began with a scene of chaos, shouting and excitement with a reddened sky in the background. The peasants were highly charged. The audience saw Panchanani or Matangini Hazra in action. They could feel the suspense in the very first scene and appreciate the technical brilliance of the set-up.

The second scene was set in the Sammaddar household. Pradhan is the eldest of the Samaddar brothers and head of the family. Kunja is Radhika's husband. Makhan is their son. Niranjan is the youngest of the Samaddar brothers and his wife is Binodini. The Samaddars were a well-off peasant household who have now lost all their wealth. Radhika uses her feet to sift through the last morsels of rice, as she begins speaking her lines. We had rehearsed the scene very well, so I wasn't too nervous about it. As scene after scene rolled out, the audience got engrossed in the action. It seemed they were attentively watching a new kind of performance. During the interval, someone came in to report that the audience reception was very positive. We found a lot of courage to complete the play. Curtains dropped. Many members of the audience visited us backstage to congratulate us. The kind of reception that we received on that day is unforgettable. It was a completely new experience for me. I got the realization that I too was an artist. After that, the play was performed for six more nights at Srirangam Theatre.

This performance sent down tremors through the Bengali theatre establishment. The old-styled practitioners were alarmed by the new production. They were apprehensive that the established theatres would suffer financially, which is why Shishirbabu refused to rent out the theatre to us again. Not only Shishirbabu, but no professional theatre was willing to rent out their stage to us. But the floodgates had been opened and there was no stopping the IPTA. The professional stage had to follow the new ideas which the IPTA had brought to the Bengali stage. Very soon, Tulsi Lahiri's *Dukhir Iman* (Pride of the Poor) was performed at Srirangam Theatre. But, as Bijonbabu had stated in the introduction to *Nabanna*—Shishir Kumar did not perform in that play. It was perhaps difficult for the 'emperor' of the Bengali stage to climb down to the level of his subjects and perform in a new kind of play. Soon, however, the emperor passed away. And with that an old era set and a new era dawned with the coming of Nabanatya.

Nabanna created history—in theatre techniques, production, subject matter and group effort. The experience of the collective acting was a novelty. We did not have actors of great stature like Shishir Kumar, Nirmalbabu or Danibabu among us, but working together made us more effective than them. We did not have any separate identity of our own, we shared our collective identity. That is the lesson which we learnt.

We kept on running along roads, by the river banks and across fields. Wherever we went we received tremendous love from the people. We enjoyed performing in front of urban educated audiences. We had much greater enjoyment while performing before one lakh strong audience of peasants at Hatgobindopur. In a performance illumined with dock lights, the swaying of one lakh heads was inspirational.

That inspiration still keeps us going. This journey should not stop. The day it does should also be the day on which the curtain falls on my journey on earth.

Memories[115]

Tripti Mitra

I do not know if there were any theatres outside Calcutta, in the rural parts of Bengal. We did have one at Thakurgaon—George Coronation Theatre. It was constructed at the time of the coronation of George V. It had a raised stage. The seats in the front rows were dug into a pit. The seats at the rear would be raised into a slope. It had a balcony as well where usually the women were seated. The theatre hosted performances regularly. My father did not visit the theatre at all. My mother enjoyed the theatre and visited it often. When I was a little child, I did visit the theatre with my mother. But I did not get to watch the overnight performances—for I used to fall asleep. Plays like *Chand Saudagar* (Chand, the Merchant), *Karagar* (Dungeon), *Savitri Satyaban*, *Shahjahan* would be performed. There were a few social plays as well, like—*Bish Bochhor Aage* (Twenty Years Ago). Most of the actors depended on other jobs during the day for their living. One of the actors was Sachida. A lawyer by profession, he performed very well in female roles. He could carry off women's attire really well. Once an old man had a great desire to get married. It was suggested that he get married to Sachida—who was presented before him in female costume. The old man liked the 'girl' and gave some money to seal the 'match'. Sachida and his friends partied with the money.

Nirmal Pal worked in a bank. He had a limp in one of his legs. But he carried off the limp with style on stage. Nalini Palit was a good actor. He performed the roles of Chand Saudagar and Ram. Even after I was introduced to the Calcutta stage, I considered them to be very good actors. Shows at the George Coronation Theatre were mostly performed by local actors. There were no shows by troupes from Calcutta or other parts of Bengal.

I came to Calcutta towards the end of 1938. I did perform in a couple of plays at school but not in too many performances. I had a lot of hair and could not manage all of it. So my mother would cut my hair short or shave my head. So I would not be considered for acting at school.

In Calcutta, we used to live with my uncle Satyen Majumdar. Bijon Bhattacharya used to come there quite often. At that time he used to write poetry and stories. *Agoon* (Fire) was his first play. Rehearsals for *Agoon* were on. I was not involved. I had never thought that I would become an actor. It was 1943. I was waiting for the results of class X exams. All of a sudden, a girl from among the actors performing *Agoon* stopped coming for rehearsals. There were just seven days to go for the first performance. Goshthoda [Bijon Bhattacharya] was in great trouble. In those days it was very difficult to find women who would act in the theatre. I did not have any desire to try acting. I was uncomfortable with the idea that I had to work with male actors. My sister (Shanti Debi—Arun Mitra's wife) spoke to me. She explained, 'If you don't act Goshthoda and the others would be in tremendous difficulty.' It was then that I took up the role of the quarrelsome wife in *Agoon*.

The rehearsals were held at 46 Dharmatala Street. I did not feel too comfortable during the rehearsals. I would be nervous. I was the youngest in the group. The others were much elder to me. There were different sorts of people there. One or two of them remarked, 'She is too young to be performing on stage.' However, I knew Sujatadi well. I liked her company.

The first performance was held at Natyabharati (later Grace Cinema). This was my first performance on a public stage. It was a lengthy programme. It started with *Agoon*. This was followed by songs and dances. Goshthoda sung 'Allah myagh de paani de', 'Kastetare diyo jore shan'. That was followed by a dance performance by Nilima Sanyal. The programme ended with Benoy Ghosh's *Laboratory*. I did not act in *Laboratory* that night, but did so later, again for want of other female actors—Sujatadi was unwell. That performance was held at Gobindababu's house at Rashbehari Avenue.

The results of class X exams were out. I got an admission in Ashutosh College. There I worked as an activist with the Students Federation with great enthusiasm. I never thought that I would return to the stage. I also took up a job.

In early 1944, I was asked to perform in *Jabanbandi*. The first performance was to be held in the Star Theatre. P.C. Joshi had come to watch the show. I did not get a chance to speak with him. He had also seen *Nabanna* and had liked the performance. Although he did appreciate my performance, I don't know if he did so since I was the youngest of the actors. I don't remember his exact words. He used to speak very fast—I don't think I gathered everything he said. Much later, for the performance of *Dharti ke lal* in Bombay, it wasn't decided if I would travel for the performance. It was due to P.C. Joshi's initiative that I performed in Bombay.

Jabanbandi was performed in a lot of places. We had

once travelled to Dhaka. On the steamer from Goalanda to Narayanganj, I met Maharshi (Monoranjan Bhattacharya). I had seen him in rehearsals earlier—he wasn't very frequent. Being much elder and famous he also appeared to be distant. But on the steamer, he did not seem to be distant at all. I also met Manik Bandopadhyay on the steamer. Manikbabu also visited us at home—my uncle's house.

I had not informed my uncle about my theatre activities. I knew that the knowledge would not please him much. Returning after rehearsals or a performance at night I would enter the house tiptoed. One night, just as I entered home, my uncle thundered, 'So you've been engaging in theatre? Where had you gone?'

I was in shock.

My uncle's voice mellowed, 'I have heard that you are doing very well. Manik has told me. Goshtho has written *Jabanbandi* and you are acting in it!' Manikbabu's certificate had saved me.

Jabanbandi was translated into Hindi. Artists from Calcutta travelled to perform in Bombay. When he heard Goshthoda was writing a new play, Shambhu Mitra came back to Calcutta in excitement. At this time Goshthoda used to say a lot of things about Matangini Hazra, 'See how a woman faced police firing— she was fearless!' I had not realized then that this was an oral prelude to his next play. Bits and parts of *Nabanna* were read at Arun Mitra's house at Sadananda Road and at the office of *Arani* and much later at 46 Dharmatala Street. However, I wasn't a party to any reading. In *Jabanbandi*, Anu Dasgupta played the character of the mother-in-law and I played the daughter-in-law. Anu got married. So she could not perform in *Nabanna*. So we needed a new female actor. My responsibility increased. Several people advised me to quit my job. On the other hand, I was seriously considering joining the Communist Party as a whole-time activist. Others advised me to be a whole-timer with the IPTA, though I wanted to continue with the Students Federation. I used to work well with students. Niharda had just been transferred to the IPTA from the Students Federation—he was a good friend. Maybe due to a large difference in age, I was not very close to people in the IPTA. Anyway, for various reasons I joined the IPTA as a whole-timer.

As work on *Nabanna* progressed, I started enjoying theatre. Till now I had just followed instructions. It was in *Nabanna* that I could relish theatre. There is a scene in the play—after a sudden meeting with her husband in Calcutta, Binodini had to describe the experiences of the entire family—the condition of the village; dark night; Pradhan had lost his two sons, he was almost mad—while uttering those lines, it felt different, it felt good. It was while working on these lines that I developed a taste for theatre, I became passionate about the theatre. It had not happened before this.

Maharshi did not visit the rehearsals regularly. Swarnababu and Arunbabu were there almost on all days. Nirenbabu may have come once or twice—he was there for the stage rehearsal.

Lalita Biswas—George Biswas's sister—used to teach at a school in Howrah. She had played the role of 'Bengal Madonna'. She was very good. Bibha was from Barishal—she spoke with a Barishal accent. Bibha and I used to work together. I encouraged Bibha to join the theatre. Bibha does not act anymore but she does visit sometimes.

Jalad, Swarnababu's friend is a school teacher. I don't know where he is now, he got lost somewhere. I liked Manidi's presence at the rehearsal. She was known to me. She was a leader. Yet she never used her authority. I was slightly anxious the day Manidi joined the rehearsals. I was anxious because I was fond of her.

Will she be able to pull it off? We knew that she was very capable in her work. But acting wasn't what she was meant to do. Will she be able to act? As if she failed, I too would have failed. Yes! She was good! In fact, she did very well. Like in other fields, she was successful on stage as well. I was relieved.

Sovadi joined IPTA during the preparations for *Nabanna*. While I was worried about my performance on stage, Sovadi and Shambhu Mitra were relaxed. Whenever they found time they would converse in hushed tones or exchange jokes. Their jokes were so funny that I could barely control my laughter if I overheard them. I tried very hard to control. But the two of them were not perturbed.

The first performance of *Nabanna* was organized by the Peoples' Relief Committee at Srirangam. Bishwanath Bhaduri, Bimal Roy, Jyotirmoy Roy, Radhamohan Bhattacharya, Prabhat Mukhopadhyay (Station Director All India Radio, Calcutta)— were present for the first show. After seeing our blackened, drought-ridden faces Bishwanath Bhaduri had said, 'Should our girls blacken their faces? Never!' Shishir Bhaduri watched a show from the wings. Later he asked Goshthoda, 'Did you think before you wrote?'

Suddenly, *Nabanna* was a hit. No one would have imagined the extent.

We travelled to a lot of places with the plays. We performed *Jabanbandi* at Mohirampur. We had to walk through the farmlands. During the rains, the fields were flooded and there was no way to tell where the pathway was between two farms. We waded through the mud and the water. There were two children with us. They held my hands and walked along. Suddenly, one of the children slipped and fell and was covered completely in mud. I quickly picked her up.

When we travelled for performances we did not get comfortable lodging. But we did not bother about it. But the children who accompanied us did undergo a lot of hardship. I did feel sorry for them.

On another occasion, *Jabanbandi* was to be performed in Jessore by local artists, but did not have female actors. So, I was called. I went to Jessore with Buroda (Sukumar Mitra). When I went to the green room to put on the make-up for the role of the daughter-in-law, I saw that a man was dressing up as the mother-in-law. I was shocked, 'How can this be? How can a woman perform as daughter-in-law and a man as mother-in-law?' Buroda also expressed his utter surprise and said that he had known nothing about this. The other actors tried explaining to us that he was very good at performing female roles. He assured us that he was a 'good mother-in-law', that the daughter-in-law had nothing to fear. There was a scene in the play where the mother-in-law plucks lice from the daughter-in-law's hair. Nasty! But nothing could be done about it. The show had to happen. It did.

But even at the end of the show the audience did not disperse. They wanted more. At Sudhida's (Sudhi Pradhan) request, I recited a poem with all my heart and soul. At that time, for every such act it seemed to me that the prestige of the IPTA depended on me, so I would put in my heart and soul. After my recitation, someone came up and said, 'It's been ages since I've heard such excellent recitation. Please announce, I would award her a medal.' He was the famous actor Naresh Mitra. So I got a medal. I had also got a cup.

But more than the cup and the medal, I remember many faces, of people who would defy the rain and floods to come before the stage, and watch our performances intently. Their eager eyes would give us energy, would give us encouragement. That was our real 'cup' and real 'medal'.

Interview[116]

Shombhu Mitra

Chittaranjan Ghosh: When did you join the Anti-Fascist Writers' and Artsits' Association?

Shombhu Mitra: Bijon [Bhattacharya] and Benoy [Ghosh] were already there. Once or twice, Bijon had invited me to join them. But I did not manage to go. Later, Benoy invited me as well. I think Maharshi would go there whenever he could. Of course, ideologically I was against fascism.

Chittaranjan Ghosh: When did you go there the first time?

Shombhu Mitra: It is very difficult to recall the exact date. As far as I can remember, the first time I went there was to attend a conference. The conference was held in a room in the upper floor of the University Institute. At the end of the meeting, I was requested to recite a poem, which I did.

Chittaranjan Ghosh:	What were the main activities of the Association at that time?
Shombhu Mitra:	Discussions, lectures, singing. As far as I can recall, Bishnubabu was the secretary of the Association. But the Association did not have much interest in theatre, which was my main interest. I tried to encourage Bijon and Benoy, and Maharshi too, to write plays. Bijon and Benoy used to write a bit, but not plays.
Chittaranjan Ghosh:	Just a minute, sorry that I am interrupting you, but you did write stories yourself! I have read a couple of stories written by you in old issues of magazines.
Shombhu Mitra:	That's a disaster! Have you discovered my dark secret? Anyway, due to my encouragement several plays were written—*Agoon*, *Laboratory*, *Homeopathy*, *Jabanbandi* and then *Nabanna*.
Chittaranjan Ghosh:	The two of you directed *Nabanna*. What about the earlier productions?
Shombhu Mitra:	*Agoon* was directed by Bijon... perhaps. *Laboratory* and other plays by me.
Chittaranjan Ghosh:	Where was *Laboratory* first performed?
Shombhu Mitra:	At Natya Bharati, which now is Grace Cinema.
Chittaranjan Ghosh:	Some people say that *Jabanbandi* was first performed at Srirangam. But as far as I know it was first performed at the

	Star Theatre.
Shombhu Mitra:	You are correct. The first performance of *Jabanbandi* was held at the Star Theatre and not at Srirangam. On that occasion I also recited a poem, 'Madhubanshir Goli'. That day P.C. Joshi was in the audience.
Chittaranjan Ghosh:	Please tell us about the production of *Jabanbandi*.
Shombhu Mitra:	The first scene of *Jabanbandi* was performed in low light. Towards the end, Paran would pick up a fistful of soil and look in the distance. The soil would slowly slip through his fingers. This was not there in the script. The end would be prolonged. The first scene portrayed the peasants' sentimental connection to the land. So it was performed in dimmed light. The rest of the play was performed in bright light—there was great clarity—starkness—the cruelty was shown. Dirty-looking flats were kept in the background. The set was inverted.
Chittaranjan Ghosh:	Inverted? What does that mean?
Shombhu Mitra:	The frame of the set would be towards the audience. Later on, we used this technique for *Borbor Banshi* as well. However, the feelings that were inherent in the script of *Jabanbandi* could not be presented on stage for various reasons. In this regard we attained greater success

	in *Nabanna*. The Hindi production of *Jabanbandi*—*Antim Abhilash* managed to collect one lakh rupees for the Bengal relief. It was translated by Nemichand Jain. He and his wife performed in the production.
Chittaranjan Ghosh:	Please tell us something about the production of *Nabanna*.
Shombhu Mitra:	The way *Nabanna* has been printed, that wasn't the way it was performed. People of this generation—who have not seen *Nabanna*—their understanding of the play is from reading the book. The script was substantially edited for performance. Particular scenes were reduced, some others expanded, and there was some reordering of the sequence of scenes. In certain cases, instead of breaking a particular sequence across scenes, they were performed together in a longer scene. I remember that this was done towards the ending of the play. For the contemporary reader it would be difficult to imaginatively reconstruct the first production of *Nabanna*. If we had an edited script such reconstruction would have been easier. The play has an episodic character. Though we did try to consolidate the episodes and contain the fragments, the episodic character remained. The

edited play was so arranged that each scene should end in the climax of one of the episodes. This climax was heightened in the production. In the scenes following the Samaddar family's transition to Calcutta, cries of 'Phyan dao!' (A little starch water please) were sounded in the background. In the days of the famine, such desperate cries were heard all over the streets of Calcutta. At the time of the production, these cries were fresh in the minds of the audience. In the last scene, these cries were not sounded. The wedding reception scene too began with these cries—the shehnai came after that. The reception scene ends with Kunja being bitten by a dog at the dustbin. Radhika covers the wound with a rag. She says, 'Does it pain a lot?' Radhika realizes her nursing is inadequate, but what more can a beggar on the street do? With great concern and helplessness she asks, 'Do you want some water to drink? Should I get you some water? Water?' What more can she do? This incident brings back to their mind memories of home—Aminpur. They tear up. Just then the cries of 'Phyan dao' come in from the backstage and disrupt the tenderness of the moment.

Nabanna ▪ 181

The scene changes, the action moves on to the next scene. This cry for food was extremely real and fresh at that time as if the entire people were screaming for help. We prepared the set with jute cloth—a fact now known to everyone. It was low-cost design. We did not use the revolving stage for the first act. There was a single set. The first act includes a storm sequence. To create the storm, the sounds, and the image of destruction, an elaborate arrangement was required. But we did not have such an arrangement at that time. We had to show the roof collapsing, the flooding of the house. Sound had to be created and yet, the volume would have to be controlled to ensure it did not drown out the dialogues. We had wanted to have a broken branch fly onto the stage. But to do that everyday, was a big hassle. The storm darkens the sky, but in order to show the effect of the storm as well as the characters we needed light. In those days there wasn't much variety in theatre lights. There were no spots other than carbon arc. Some amount of the dialogues would be inaudible. So we stressed on the most important utterance. Pradhan (Bijon Bhattacharya) says, 'The paths have entered our home.' We did not want to use any western instruments. Western instruments were used in most films or stage events. Uday Shankar never used any western instruments in his programmes. However, we were unable to make requisite arrangements and had to use a piano. In all probability it was Sujit Nath who played it. The coming of the storm was first indicated on the piano—later other instruments would join. The stage would darken, the music would continue along with sounds of chaos and fear, Bijon would pour a bucket of water on himself before re-entering the stage, the carbon arc spotlight would be focused on him. Bijon would say, 'The paths have entered our home.' After this I would enter after having soaked myself in oil—with the spot on me it would seem as if I am drenched in water. Maharshi had advised us to create a gap between the flaps in the background. The opposite sector of the revolving stage would be vacant. The grey backdrop would not be seen. It would give the appearance of a deep darkness, an ashen lifelessness and a picture of destruction. This sector would already have a mound created in its centre. In the first scene of the play,

	this space would be lit with colour filters from floodlights to depict a reddened horizon. Dhuno[117] would be used to create smoke. In the storm scene, while pulling the flaps apart, we would remove a couple of iron rods from the frame. This gave the effect of the roof falling over.
Chittaranjan Ghosh:	Your set for the park scene was much appreciated.
Shombhu Mitra:	True. But it was very simple. We used a fence and and a bench to create it.
Chittaranjan Ghosh:	In this scene you had performed in a minor character.
Shombhu Mitra:	Yes, as a tout. In *Nabanna*, I had to perform two roles—as Dayal and as the tout. Originally the character of the tout would be performed by Prafulla Roy from Agrani. But even after several rehearsals he could not do justice to the character. So I had to step in.
Chittaranjan Ghosh:	Was the rooster fight shown in any of the performances?
Shombhu Mitra:	No. There was no rooster fight. We did show the communal farming, and the stick fight. The stick fight scene would be performed by students. Towards the end of the scene there would be a song—'*Janani go janmabhumi bandi go rani*' (Our motherland exists in shackles). Probably this song was left out in the printed

edition. The choreography during this song was beautiful. Downstage, the women would carry a lamp on their heads while singing. There would be no light on them. The floodlights would light up the upstage from the wings. This would create a silhouette. The flames would shiver on the heads of the women. It was a very pretty sight. In those days no one used the silhouette. The technician whom we asked to light up the background from the wings was thoroughly amazed—'Are you sure? Should I not throw the light on the actors?' The clinic was also created with great simplicity. A table and a few chairs. In the background, hung a red banner—'Charity Clinic'.

Chittaranjan Ghosh: What was the quality of the acting?

Shombhu Mitra: Most of the actors were new. They lacked voice training. But that was good enough for playing peasant characters. If I told them, 'Raise your voice', they would raise their voice. Peasants do speak in a loud tone. The actors would think they are being loud, but that did not reach the audience. It would seem fine. The actors who did have voice training, we would give them bhadralok characters to perform—ARP, Civic Guard and others.

Chittaranjan Ghosh: Where lies the importance of *Nabanna*?

Shombhu Mitra: *Nabanna* could encapsulate the pain of the people of the time. Before *Nabanna*, there were many family dramas performed on the Bengali stage. In *Nabanna*, the crisis in the family has as its basis a social crisis. The play is episodic—at least some or the other of its parts touched everyone—the people, the entire country. Even untrained voices fell into place. In a situation of heightened tension—refugees in a city, away from home, away from their village—in such desperate condition, it is probable that the peasants would speak in a voice cast out of tune, bereft of any sophistication. The events of the play were very relevant, very real for the audience, and it did not require much effort for them to react. And the realization that theatre can tell a different kind of story, and the production techniques could be different—this realization began with *Nabanna*.

Cast
First Performance: Srirangam 24 October 1944

Pradhan Samaddar	Bijon Bhattacharya
Kunja Samaddar	Sudhi Pradhan
Niranjan Samaddar	Jalad Chattapadhyay
Makhan	Monika Bhattacharya (Chakraborty)
Panchanani	Manikutala Sen
Radhika	Sova Sen
Binodini	Tripti Bhaduri (Mitra)
Dayal Mondol	Shombhu Mitra
Haru Dutta	Gangapada Basu
Kalidhan Dhara	Charuprakash Ghosh
Rajib	Sajal Roychowdhury
Chander	Ranjit Basu
Judhisthir	Nihar Dasgupta
Photographers	Amal Bhattacharya
	Robin Majumdar
First bhadralok	Monoronjon Baral
Barakorta	Chitto Hore
Aged beggar	Gopal Haldar
Dom	Sambhu Haldar
Inspector	Bimalendu Ghosh
Doctor	Samar Roychoudhary
Digambar	Ajit Mitra
Fakir	Satyajiban Bhattacharya
Khuki's mother	Kalyani Kumaramangalam

Beggar	Bibha Sen
Bengal Madonna	Lalita Biswas

Bhadralok, Nirmal, Tout, Beggar, Haru Dutta's brother-in-law, Constable, Patient, Servant, Chander's daughter, Barkat, Farmer, starving people, crowds.

Produced by:	Indian People's Theatre Association
Directed by:	Shombhu Mitra and Bijon Bhattacharya
Advisor:	Manoranjan Bhattacharya
Music Director:	Gaur Ghosh
Assistants:	Sujit Nath, Sushil Biswas, Ardhendu Ghosh, Barada Gupta
	Bijoy Dey, Sunil Gupta
	Khirod Ganguly, Shanti Mitra
	Shailen Das, Kamal Mitra
	Nanigopal Chaudury
	Chandi Ghosh, Lakhan Das
Stage Manager:	Chitto Banerjee
Assisted by:	Arun Dasgupta

Bibliography

Abbas, Khwaja Ahmed. *Antim Abhilash*. *Bohurupee: Nabanna Special Issue (First Issue)*, no. 33 (1969): 99–100.

Ahmed, A.W. Nuruddin, and Lutful Hoq Chowdhury. 'History of the Ministry of Food'. International Food Policy Research Institute, Bangladesh Food Policy Project, June 1994. http://pdf.usaid.gov/pdf_docs/PNABS149.pdf.

Bandopadhyay, Manik. 'Bharater Marmabani' [The Heart of India]'. *Rangapat Natyapatra: Bijon Bhattacharya Special Issue*, no. 10 (n.d.): 48–49.

Bandopadhyay, Tarashankar. 'Manwantar o Sahitya' [Famine and Literature]'. *Bohurupee: Nabanna Special Issue (First Issue)*, no. 33 (n.d.): 118.

Bandopadhyaya, Samik. 'Bijon Bhattacharya'. *Sayak Natyapatra: Noboparjaye*, no. 1 (November 2001): 3–12.

———. 'Nabanna Prasange' (About Nabanna)'. In *Nabanna*, by Bijon Bhattacharya, 7–19. Kolkata: Dey's Publishing, 2008.

———. 'Nabanna-r- Dhara Theke Onyo Dharaye: Ekta Osompurna Alochona' (Legacy of Nabanna and Other Legacies: An Incomplete Discussion).' *Bohurupee: Nabanna Special Issue (Second Issue)*, no. 34 (June 1970): 86–100.

———. 'Theatrescapes.' *Seagull Theatre Quarterly*, no. 16 (1997): 25–30.

Banerjee, Chitto. 'Nabanna: Mancher Nepatthye' [Nabanna: Behind the Scenes.]'. *Bohurupee: Nabanna Special Issue (First Issue)*, no. 33 (1969): 164–65.

Basu, Gangapada. 'Nabanna-r Aage' [Before Nabanna]'. *Bohurupee: Nabanna Special Issue (First Issue)*, no. 33 (1969): 142–47.

Bhatia, Nandi. *Acts of Authority, Acts of Resistance: Theater and Politics in Colonial and Postcolonial India*. New Delhi: Oxford University Press, 2004.

———. 'Staging Resistance: The Indian People's Theatre Association'. In *The Politics of Culture in the Shadow of Capital*, edited by Lisa Lowe and David Lloyd. Durham, NC: Duke University Press, 1997.

Bhattacharya, Bijon. 'Jabanbandi'. In *Bijon Bhattacharya Rachana Samgraha*, edited by Nabarun Bhattacharya and Samik Bandopadhyaya, One: 13–30. Kolkata: Dey's Publishing, 2008.

———. 'Nabanna-r Natyakarer Protibedon' (Presentation by the Playwright of Nabanna). In *Nabanna*, 122–24. Kolkata: Dey's Publishing, 2008.

Bhattacharya, Malini. 'The Indian People's Theatre Association: A Preliminary Sketch of the Movement and the Organization 1942 47'. *Sangeet Natak*, no. 94 (December 1989): 3–21.

———. 'The IPTA in Bengal'. *Journal of Arts and Ideas*, no. January–March (1983): 5–22.

Bhattacharya, Tapas. *Bijon Bhattacharya, Gananatya Andolon o Nabanna Ebong'* [Bijon Bhattacharya, People's Theatre Movement and Nabanna]. Kolkata: Jatiya Sahitya Parishad, 2001.

Biswas, Kalpana, and Mahendra Kumar. 'Bijon Bhattacharya: Interview'. *Bohurupee*, no. 49 (1978): 34–48.

Bose, Sugata, and Ayesha Jalal. *Modern South Asia: History, Culture, Political Economy*. London and New York: Routledge, 2001.

Chakraborty, Himachal. 'Bijon Bhattacharya-r Natok' [Bijon Bhattacharya's Plays]'. *Korok*, no. Sharod (2013): 180–92.

Chakravarty, Gargi. 'Famine, Food and the Politics of Survival in Calcutta: 1943-50'. In *Calcutta: The Stormy Decades*, by Tanika Sarkar and Sekhar Bandopadhyay, 204–28. New York and Oxon: Routledge, 2018.

Chattopadhyay, Sunil. 'Anjangarh and Kerani Natoker Bhumika' [Anjangarh and Kerani: Introduction to Two Plays]. *Bohurupee: Nabanna Special Issue (First Issue)*, no. 33 (1969): 127–30.

Datta, Partho. 'Calcutta on the Threshold of the 1940s.' In *Calcutta: The Stormy Decades*, by Tanika Sarkar and Sekhar Bandopadhyay, 18–41.

Ghatak, Ritwik. 'Bijon Bhattarcharya: Jiboner Sutradhar' [Bijon Bhattacharya: Narrator of Life]'. *Natyadarpan*, no. 1 (1975): 13–15.

———. *On the Cultural Front: A Thesis Submitted by Ritwik Ghatak to the Communist Party of India in 1954*. Calcutta: Ritwik Memorial Trust, 2000.

Ghosh, Benoy. 'Ekpurusher Dustor Byabodhan' [Gap of a Generation]'. *Bohurupee: Nabanna Special Issue (First Issue)*, no. 33 (1969): 131–36.

Ghosh, Chittaranjan. 'Tinti Natika o Nabanna-r Prothom Smaronik' [First Souvenir of Tinti Natika and Nabanna]. *Bohurupee: Nabanna Special Issue (First Issue)*, no. 33 (1969): 87–93.

Ghosh, Nemai. 'Amar Anondo, Amar Gorbo' [My Pleasure, My Pride]'. *Bohurupee: Nabanna Special Issue (First Issue)*, no. 33 (1969): 162–63.

Kamtekar, Indivar. 'A Different War Dance: State and Class in India 1939–1945'. *Past & Present*, no. 176 (August 2002): 187–221.

Mishra, Ashok Kumar. *Gananatya Andolon o Nabanna* [The People's Theatre Movement and Nabanna]. Kolkata: Bangiya Sahitya Samsad, 2015.

Mitra, Shombhu. 'Proshner Uttare' [Answering Questions]. Interviewed by Chittaranjan Ghosh. *Bohurupee: Nabanna Special Issue (Second Issue)*, no. 34 (June 1970): 67–75.

———. 'Swagoto' [Welcome]. *Bohurupee: Nabanna Special Issue (First Issue)*, no. 33 (1969): 174–76.

Mitra, Tripti. 'Purono Kotha' [Memories]. *Bohurupee: Nabanna Special Issue (First Issue)*, no. 33 (1969): 188–93.

Mukherjee, Janam. 'Japan Attacks'. In *Calcutta: The Stormy Decades*, by Tanika Sarkar and Sekhar Bandopadhyay, 93–120.

Mukhopadhyay, Subhash. 'Nabanner Aage' [Before Nabanna]. *Bohurupee: Nabanna Special Issue (First Issue)*, no. 33 (1969): 137–41.

Pradhan, Sudhi. *Marxist Cultural Movement in India: Chronicles and Documents*. Vol. 1. Calcutta: Santi Pradhan, 1985.

Pradhan, Sudhi, Sova Sen, Sajal Roychowdhury, and Tripti Mitra. *Discussion on (Nabanna) by the Original Cast*, 1992.

Rahim, N.K. 'Dharti Ke Lal'. *Bohurupee: Nabanna Special Issue (First Issue)*, no. 33 (1969): 125.

Sarkar, Sumit. *Modern India, 1885–1947*. Delhi: Macmillan, 1983.

Sen, Amartya. *Poverty and Famines: An Essay on Entitlement and Development*. Oxford: Clarendon Press, 1981.

Sen, Ashok. 'Shombhu Mitra: Abhinoyer Kichhu Smriti' [Shombhu Mitra: Reminiscences from the Stage]. *Bohurupee*, no. 83 (May 1995): 87–93.

Sen, Sova. 'Nabanna o Aami' [Nabanna and Me]'. *Bohurupee: Nabanna*

Special Issue (First Issue), no. 33 (1969): 148–51.

Sengupta, Debjani. 'A Metropolis of Hunger: Calcutta's Poetry of the Famine (1943)'. *Coldnoon* (blog), 7 August 2016. http://coldnoon.com/a-metropolis-of-hunger-calcuttas-poetry-of-the-famine-1943/.

Tharoor, Shashi. 'The Ugly Briton'. Time.com, 26 September 2017. http://content.time.com/time/magazine/article/0,9171,2031992,00.html.

Endnotes

1. Sumit Sarkar, *Modern India*, pp. 407–8.
2. Nandi Bhatia, *Acts of Authority, Acts of Resistance: Theater and Politics in Colonial and Postcolonial India*, p. 82; Malini Bhattacharya, 'The IPTA in Bengal,' pp. 8–12; also see Malini Bhattacharya, 'The Indian People's Theatre Association: A Preliminary Sketch of the Movement and the Organization 1942–47,' p. 17; Nandi Bhatia, 'Staging Resistance: The Indian People's Theatre Association,' pp. 433–39.
3. Partho Datta, 'Calcutta on the Threshold of the 1940s,' pp. 18–41.
4. Indivar Kamtekar, 'A Different War Dance: State and Class in India 1939-1945,' p. 189.
5. Amartya Sen, *Poverty and Famines: An Essay on Entitlement and Development*, p. 58; Ashok Kumar Mishra, *Gananatya Andolon o Nabanna* [The People's Theatre Movement and Nabanna], p. 18.
6. Sen writes, 'In 1942 the autumn crop was a little less than normal (97% of the preceding four years), and the winter crop quite a bit less (83% of the average preceding four years). This was largely the result of a cyclone in October, followed by torrential rain in some parts of Bengal and a subsequent fungus disease... The current supply for 1943 was only about 5% lower than the average of the preceding five years. It was, in fact, 13% higher than in 1941, and there was, of course, no famine in 1941.' See Sen, *Poverty and Famines: An Essay on Entitlement and Development*, pp. 52–58.
7. Mishra, *Gananatya Andolon o Nabanna*, p. 18; Janam Mukherjee, 'Japan Attacks,' p. 94.

8. Kamtekar, 'A Different War Dance: State and Class in India 1939–1945,' p. 188.
9. Sen, *Poverty and Famines: An Essay on Entitlement and Development*, p. 78.
10. Gargi Chakravarty, 'Famine, Food and the Politics of Survival in Calcutta: 1943–50,' pp. 208–25.
11. Sugata Bose and Ayesha Jalal, *Modern South Asia: History, Culture, Political Economy*, p. 158.
12. Kamtekar, 'A Different War Dance: State and Class in India 1939–1945,' p. 212; Sen, *Poverty and Famines: An Essay on Entitlement and Development*, p. 58.
13. Sen, *Poverty and Famines: An Essay on Entitlement and Development*, p. 57.
14. Ibid., p. 73.
15. Chakravarty, 'Famine, Food and the Politics of Survival in Calcutta: 1943–50,' p. 225.
16. Mishra, *Gananatya Andolon o Nabanna*, p. 51.
17. Mukherjee, 'Japan Attacks,' p. 99.
18. Shashi Tharoor, 'The Ugly Briton.'
19. Mukherjee, 'Japan Attacks,' p. 94.
20. Sarkar, *Modern India, 1885–1947*, p. 385.
21. Gangapada Basu, 'Nabanne-r Aage,' p. 143.
22. Sarkar, *Modern India, 1885–1947*, p. 413.
23. Sudhi Pradhan, *Marxist Cultural Movement in India: Chronicles and Documents*, vol. 1, p. 6.
24. Sudhi Pradhan et al., *Discussion on [Nabanna] by the Original Cast*, 1992.
25. Basu, 'Nabanner Aage,' p. 143.
26. Sunil Chattopadhyay, 'Anjangarh and Kerani Natoker Bhumika. pp. 127–30.
27. Ibid., p. 131.
28. Mishra, *Gananatya Andolon o Nabanna*.
29. Subhash Mukhopadhyay, 'Nabanner Aage' p. 137.
30. Benoy Ghosh, 'Ekpurusher Dustor Byabodhan' p. 134.
31. Ashok Sen, 'Shombhu Mitra: Abhinoyer Kichhu Smriti, p. 110.
32. Mukhopadhyay, 'Nabanner Aage,' p. 139.
33. Ghosh, 'Ekpurusher Dustor Byabodhan,' p. 132; Mukhopadhyay, 'Nabanner Aage,' p. 137.
34. Shombhu Mitra, 'Proshner Uttare' p. 71.
35. Khwaja Ahmed Abbas, 'Antim Abhilash,' p. 100.

36. Samik Bandopadhyaya, 'Nabanna-r Dhara Theke Onyo Dharaye: Ekta Osompurna Alochona,' p. 88.
37. Kalpana Biswas and Mahendra Kumar, 'Bijon Bhattacharya: Interview,' p. 13.
38. Chakravarty, 'Famine, Food and the Politics of Survival in Calcutta: 1943–50,' pp. 218–21.
39. Quoted in Debjani Sengupta, 'A Metropolis of Hunger: Calcutta's Poetry of the Famine (1943).'
40. Himachal Chakraborty, 'Bijon Bhattacharya-r Natok,' p. 183.
41. Bijon Bhattacharya, 'Jabanbandi,' in Bijon Bhattacharya Rachana Samgraha, ed. Nabarun Bhattacharya and Samik Bandopadhyaya, pp. 13–30.
42. *Anandabazar Patrika* 7 January 1944. Quoted in Chittaranjan Ghosh, 'Tinti Natika o Nabanna-r Prothom Smaronik,' pp. 87–93. My translation.
43. Bhattacharya, 'The IPTA in Bengal,' p. 10.
44. Sen, 'Shombhu Mitra: Abhinoyer Kichhu Smriti,' p. 92.
45. Mitra, 'Proshner Uttare', p. 72.
46. Chattopadhyay, 'Anjangarh and Kerani Natoker Bhumika,' p. 128.
47. Ritwik Ghatak, 'Bijon Bhattarcharya: Jiboner Sutradhar,' p. 13.
48. Mishra, *Gananatya Andolon o Nabanna*, p. 9.
49. Ghosh, 'Tinti Natika o Nabanna-r Prothom Smaronik,' p. 91.
50. Samik Bandopadhyaya, 'Bijon Bhattacharya,' p. 4.
51. Mishra, *Gananatya Andolon o Nabanna*, p. 68.
52. Basu, 'Nabanna-r Aage,' p. 144.
53. Bandopadhyaya, 'Nabanna-r Dhara Theke Onyo Dharaye: Ekta Osompurna Alochona,' p. 92.
54. Bijon Bhattacharya: 'Some said you have villified the Congress. I said, where have we villified anyone? There is a universal struggle. Nobody is vilifying anybody. I am not a man of any party. I only have my people.... I am defending the cause... Much brickbats and rotten eggs and vegetable were thrown at us. We were harassed a lot... I told the artists, Bear it. Go on. Don't mind the brickbats. Bleed, but don't leave the stage till the performance is over.' Biswas and Kumar, 'Bijon Bhattacharya: Interview,' p. 46.
55. Unfortunately, this draconian legislation is valid in independent India even today.

56. 'I had to fight with my whole heart. In my personal case I had to go to the Lalbazar many times when I was doing *Nabanna*. I had to fight with the Assistant Police Commissioner over every point. I had to argue with him.' Biswas and Kumar, 'Bijon Bhattacharya: Interview,' p. 45.

57. Bijon Bhattacharya, 'Nabanna-r Natyakarer Protibedon,' in *Nabanna*, p. 123.

58. Basu, 'Nabanna-r Aage,' p. 145; Sova Sen, 'Nabanna o Aami,' p. 150.

59. Bandopadhyaya, 'Bijon Bhattacharya,' p. 5.

60. Shombhu Mitra, 'Swagoto,' p. 175; Chitto Banerjee, 'Nabanna: Mancher Nepattye,' p. 165.

61. Pradhan et al., Discussion on [Nabanna] by the Original Cast.

62. Basu, 'Nabanna-r Aage,' p. 145.

63. The first round of performances were held at Srirangam in 1944 on 24 and 27 October and 10, 13, 14, 17 and 20 November. Ghosh, 'Tinti Natika o Nabanna-r Prothom Smaronik,' p. 89.

64. Mishra, *Gananatya Andolon o Nabanna*, p. 78.

65. Shombhu Mitra mentions that in performance the scenes were rearranged to ensure each change of set ends in a climax and that this altered sequence is not the same as that of the printed version of the play. However, I have not come across this version of events from any other source. Mitra, 'Proshner Uttare', p. 73.

66. Mitra, p. 73.

67. Shombhu Mitra said, 'We did not wish to use any Western instruments. Such instruments were used by all cinema and theatre productions. But Uday Shankar never used any western instrument during his programmes. But we were unable to make proper arrangements. Hence, we used the piano. Mitra, 'Proshner Uttare', p. 74.

68. Mitra, 'Proshner Uttare', p. 75.

69. Basu, 'Nabanna-r Aage,' p. 146.

70. Sen, 'Nabanna o Aami,' p. 151.

71. Tapas Bhattacharya and Bijon Bhattacharya, *Gananatya Andolon o Nabanna Ebong*.

72. Nemai Ghosh, 'Amar Anondo, Amar Gorbo,' p. 163.

73. Manik Bandopadhyay, 'Bharater Marmabani,' p. 48; Tarashankar Bandopadhyay, 'Manwantar o Sahitya,' p. 119.

74. Sudhi Pradhan quotes a report presented by Charuprakash Ghose on

behalf of the CPI Cell within the Bengal IPTA which records that one of the reasons for the IPTA abandoning Nabanna was that the co-director Shombhu Mitra 'would not agree to stage Nabanna on fixed type boards. He insisted on the revolving type stage as otherwise, he feared, it would not be possible to maintain the tempo of the drama. The result was, we had to suspend all activities'. However, Shombhu Mitra notes in an interview, 'I felt if we did good plays people will like them. Which is why I wanted to perform in Srirangam again. That stage had depth.' Pradhan, *Marxist Cultural Movement in India: Chronicles and Documents*, vol. 1, p. 325; Sen, 'Shombhu Mitra: Abhinoyer Kichhu Smriti.'

75. Ghosh, 'Amar Anondo, Amar Gorbo,' p. 163.
76. Banerjee, 'Nabanna: Mancher Nepattye,' 165; Sen, 'Nabanna o Aami,' p. 151.
77. Pradhan et al., Discussion on [Nabanna] by the Original Cast.
78. N.K. Rahim, 'Dharti Ke Lal,' p. 125.
79. Samik Bandopadhyaya, 'Theatrescapes,' p. 26.
80. Ritwik Ghatak, *On the Cultural Front: A Thesis Submitted by Ritwik Ghatak to the Communist Party of India in 1954*.
81. Sen, 'Shombhu Mitra: Abhinoyer Kichhu Smriti,' p. 93.
82. Quoted in Bandopadhyaya, 'Nabanna Prasange,' in *Nabanna*, p. 13.
83. Played by Shombhu Mitra.
84. At the beginning of the play, before the curtain rises, a voice-over—in this case that of Shombhu Mitra—announces '1942, 9th August'.
85. There is no clear indication in the play about who Shripati and Bhupati are. However, they may be assumed to be Pradhan's sons who were killed during the police repression of the August movement.
86. An enclosure made of cane or bamboo, used to store paddy.
87. Uncle
88. Aunt
89. A variety of rice.
90. In the face of a threat of Japanese invasion in March 1942, the British government announced a 'Denial Policy' to prevent any foodgrains or means of transport from falling into the hands of the enemy. Surplus stocks of paddy were burnt and boats and other means of transport were destroyed or dislocated.
91. As part of the 'Denial Policy' boats had to be destroyed or dislocated.

92. A description of the performance of the storm sequence can be found in the 'Interview' of Shombhu Mitra included in this volume.
93. A cotton cloth used as a towel or garment.
94. A refrain that is uttered by bearers of a hearse.
95. 'O Mother'
96. The end of the saree that is left loose or wrapped around.
97. Medicine prepared by boiling certain herbs.
98. A person who burns the dead at the burning ghats; usually a profession determined by caste.
99. A dish prepared by boiling rice and lentils.
100. A deity.
101. Usually these scenes set in Calcutta would be interspersed with cries of 'Phyan Dao' from backstage.
102. Once the World War was declared, the British Government of India passed the Defence of India Act 1939 in September 1939. This Act provided Emergency powers to the government to hold trials without appeal. When the food crisis emerged, the Bengal Rationing Order, 1943 was promulgated by the Governor General of Bengal in November 1943 under the powers delegated to the provincial government under the Defence of India Act 1939. The Rationing Order which instituted rationing system in India for the first time, prohibited the 'receipt of any rationed article from anybody other than authorized supplier'. A.W. Nuruddin Ahmed and Lutful Hoq Chowdhury, 'History of the Ministry of Food' (International Food Policy Research Institute, Bangladesh Food Policy Project, June 1994), 42a, http://pdf.usaid.gov/pdf_docs/PNABS149.pdf.
103. Under the Air Raid Precautions scheme (A.R.P.), a force was set up by the colonial government to act in case Calcutta was bombed by Japanese planes. Drafted into the A.R.P. were influential Hindu citizens who were then utilized for pro-government propaganda. However, the government found the A.R.P. useful even without bomb raids. The A.R.P. volunteers were posted at queues before control shops rationing food items to 'keep the peace'. The A.R.P. forces were provided corpse disposal vans to remove casualties from the air raids. When the famine came, the A.R.P. used these vans to forcibly remove the famine victims—if alive, to repatriation camps outside Calcutta and if dead, to burial grounds or crematoriums.

Clearly, the A.R.P. volunteers represented the colonial order—the partnership between the British rulers and their Indian collaborators. See Janam Mukherjee, 'Japan Attacks,' pp. 102–03.

104. It is generally believed that the Chatak bird waits for the rain to quench its thirst.
105. Landlord
106. Moneylender.
107. Sister-in-law
108. A unit to measure land area in the Indian subcontinent.
109. A sweet dish prepared with rice powder and shredded coconut which is usually prepared with freshly harvested rice on the occasion of Makar Sankranti. Makar Sankranti is celebrated differently across the subcontinent—here in the form of the harvest festival—Nabanna.
110. A sweet dish prepared by frying flour batter in spiral shapes and soaking them in sugar syrup.
111. Head of the village. Here used as an affectionate term.
112. Translated from Bijon Bhattacharya, 'Nabanna-r Natyakarer Protibedon,' in Nabanna pp. 122–24. This speech was made at a function to commemorate twenty-five years of the performance of *Nabanna*.
113. 'di' is a suffix for 'didi' or 'elder sister'. Here it is used as a term denoting respect.
114. Translated from Sen, 'Nabanna o Aami,' pp. 148–51.
115. Translated from Tripti Mitra, 'Purono Kotha,' pp. 188–93.
116. Extract. Translated from Shombhu Mitra, 'Proshner Uttare,' pp. 67–75.
117. Incense smoke

Acknowledgements

This book emerged out of a need to teach and to introduce students to the magical period of the birth of the IPTA, the coming of age of modern Indian theatre. The text developed over several semesters of engagement in the classroom. This would not have been possible without the insights offered by my students. Simona Sawhney included a draft of the translation as part of her course. Her feedback encouraged me to make the text available for the wider world. I am grateful to Samik Bandopadhyay for reading a very early draft of my essay on *Nabanna*. This work has benefited immensely from his vast knowledge of Indian theatre. Hunting through the archives was made easier by the staff of the Natya Shodh Sansthan and the National Library in Kolkata. A special mention must be made of the tireless librarian Ashim Mukherjee whom generations of scholars would remember for helping them navigate the vast caverns of the National Library and the thickness of its bureaucracy.

I am grateful to Tathagata Bhattacharya, Bishnupriya Dutt and Shaoli Mitra for their generosity in allowing me to use translations of the works included in this volume. I hope I have been able to do justice to the trust that they have reposed in me.

I'd like to thank Rupa Publications for agreeing to publish this work and Elina Majumdar for believing in me.

This book was a long time coming—a journey that would not have been possible without Nilanjana and Kouroki.